Knowing the Manifestations of Ra *Again*

An Introduction to
AmenRa Spiritual Enlightenment
and
The Accompanying Physical Energy Management System of A RA
(a Kamitic Energy system)

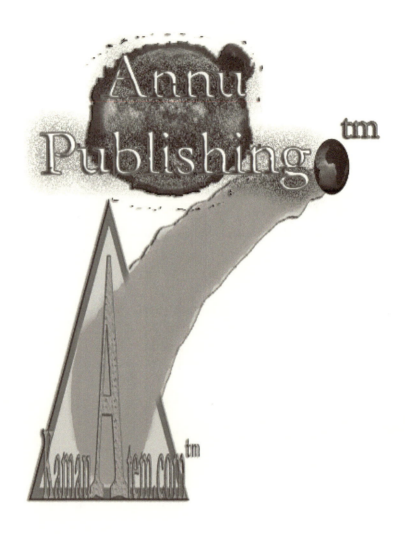

Copyright 2006 by Annu Publishing.
All Rights Reserved.
ISBN: 978-1-4303-1836-1
No part of this book may be reprinted,
Or copied in any way with out express
Permission from the author, publisher.

The Book Of Knowing The Manifestations of Ra *Again*

DISCLAIMER

This is a book of faith. As such the author does not warrant the success any person would have using any of the techniques contained herein. Success and failure will vary. There are several exercises and supplements in this book. No one should undertake any exercise or supplement program with out consulting a physician.

The Book Of Knowing The Manifestations of Ra *Again*

Author's Note

　　While this book concerns one of the greatest spiritual systems, AmenRa Enlightenment, and its accompanying energy management system (martial art) named A RA-(Aw Ra) ever known to man, there is no plead for violence nor any need for such. And make no mistake, it is great because its practitioners strive to deny the things of the world above all else while becoming as physically strong as possible. Now, any individual who reads this work believing that it calls for any war or other physical confrontation in the name of any God has not understood the meaning or the intent of the work.
　　You see this book is intended for the height of service in God's work upon the earth. The intent is no more than to create spiritually strong individuals who can do the work needed to unify people, who can teach other people to love each other; all while suffering those of us still upon the earth who have not grown strong enough to let go the faint heart and all the other emotional bondage which creates the misery and war and strife and disease and starvation and poverty and waste and...on this planet. There is no Jihad or any other such so called external holy war here. No offensive

The Book Of Knowing The Manifestations of Ra *Again*

(without actual real threat) physical blow can ever be struck righteously in the name of AmenRa while using A Ra. However, it is the work for God which will empower the practitioner to commit the great miracles while practicing the management system. No, there is no war here.

But there are two great battles here. There is one within the practitioner while he fights within himself to over come the illusion of separateness and emotionality which will keep him from becoming a better human being (read spiritually stronger) and then there is the battle of the practitioner who becomes an adept with those who would keep the adept from helping the world to be a better place when the adept helps others understand that illusion of separateness and emotionality in his efforts of unification of the world. In this second battle, it is only the spirit of the adept which fights on planes unseen by human eyes against forces which the untrained believe either don't exist or can't be fought. The adept knows that a single blow struck or myriad blows thrown would never undo what has been created within the collective spirit of those who stand against unity and love, the essence of spirituality, on this planet.

Lastly, there is combat here. Glorious strength of will and spirit pitted against challenges to be overcome. Here you will learn how to love and that love will become a glowing force within your spirit. That love will become the power within you that you can heal yourself and others and literally project out of your body to shield you, to strike an opponent who attacks you, to stop an opponent in his tracks before he can attack you. And none of these methods will work if they are used offensively; for that is the method God chooses to control this energy management system. Understand this is called an energy management system because you will be taught how to manage your internal spirit to become an external force. This is the highest level of martial arts, made easy between these pages. But it is a holistic system. Once you achieve It, then you will be a spectator watching within your own body as you watch the punch that your body blocks without attempting, willing to block. You will punch at people and they will feel the energy of your punch without the fist ever touching them. They will hit you and skid on your body as they strike the energy shield around your body and the hardest thrown punch will feel light as softly thrown pillow. But all of your own ability will start with how much love is in your heart....to heal the world. This is the truth behind the ancient martial arts saying that the power to hurt is the power to heal. Lastly, this is a culture and system of love. As such it is not relegated to white, black or purple people. All are welcome to practice love and give rise to strength. Amen.

The Book Of Knowing The Manifestations of Ra *Again*

THE BOOK OF KNOWING THE MANIFESTATIONS OF RA AGAIN

FORWARD

Simply put, the world is full of destruction and destroying itself. This is the perception of the spiritualist who views this planet of the 21st century. Good has not overtaken evil as the cries of the homeless and unfed combat the unheard shouts of the populace caught in war zones across the world for attention. As brother does not help sister all around us, the world is destroyed and being destroyed in every act of love not committed. Change will only come when we decide as one to truly love each other and give according to each other's needs with no thought for our own self.

This is the answer to every question asked every politician across the world regarding any problem in any situation faced by any government. Only a spiritual solution will suffice. Anything less is a standoff with Set's minions--those who worship any thing above God the almighty, those who worship money and power over the world and use those of us with weak life force to perpetuate that struggle, that worship.

What has this to do with this Book of Knowing the Manifestations of Ra? It is the reason for its creation thousands of years ago, the reason why

The Book Of Knowing The Manifestations of Ra *Again*

God has allowed me to deliver it to you now. The original Book was a tome to the foul state of the world and its healing (or destruction) written around 322 B.C. and one of the greatest works left by the people known as the Egyptians. By now most any spiritualist who has over come his own lower animal knows that the great people who devoted themselves and their culture to God the hidden and concealed--Amen--and the spiritual strength to live as God would upon the earth--Ra!(Life!Health!Strength!)--did not worship the sun nor did they worship many Gods nor objects just as Christians do not worship wooden crosses and three different deities called the Father, the Son, and the Holy Ghost. No, enough has been written so that we now know that these people used the things around them to cultivate themselves and have conversations about God so that every one could become part of One... The so called myths about Mighty Ra (Life! Health! Strength!) were known by all as well as the great triumph of Heru over his evil uncle Set who had succumbed to temptation (as his counterpart Lucifer would in the latter version called the Bible) was known by all so that a spiritual teacher could say to the student, "be Heru over come the Set within or Be Ra! (Life!Health!Strength!) Llead souls away from the horde of Set and past the Apep serpent to the blessed fields of Amen-ta--peace and harmony." This is no different from the "what would Jesus do" movement sweeping Christianity. The stories were mere tools, the canvas was the soul of the spiritualist, the subject was the listener's soul, the reason for the telling,--God reflecting itself as only It can in the peace and harmony within and without.

    With this book--a reinterpretation, and retelling of the ancient body of work known as The Theology of Ra, you will learn how to create yourself into a tool for God's Kingdom upon the earth. This is dangerous work and failure waits in every task failed, every test denied. It will take great strength of hope and faith and physical power...It will take spiritual greatness. You will deny yourself for the majority's needs. You will give until you are no more. (Is it not said that Maat-true love- is the Food and Drink of Ra!) And in this great struggle you will gain...You will loose. But you will grow until you no longer know you but only God.

    And upon that day, you will be one of the most powerful beings on the planet. But this will not matter for the world will hold nothing for you. Am I telling you that you will be so powerful that God will allow you to close your eyes and see the death of the true killers of the world--the minions of Set hidden behind politician and business man labels (who are they if they knowingly sell you death and bleed you dry for the love of their own hoarding of the world's resources, but the legs of the giant serpent Apep?) --

The Book Of Knowing The Manifestations of Ra *Again*

and those people would die? Perhaps, but by the time that you attain this power you would only use it if it is Gods will. At any rate, you would only use that power if it were God's will because there would be no other for you. Or you would not have The Power and it would not work..

We are talking about a systemic approach to becoming The Power in humanity against which no weapon can prosper and for which only purified soul can stand. But the way is perilous and wrought with danger. Please, please, oh please believe me. Failure to achieve the end once this system is undertaken could lead to the death of your immortal soul upon earth. This is why this was once kept secret and hence one of the greatest mysteries of the mystery systems. Understand this is perhaps one of the greatest spiritual systems the world has ever known, yet the cost of failure is perhaps the ultimate loss. We shall see how by the end of the work. But KNOW THIS: IF YOU FAIL TO COMPLETE THE PURIFICATION OF YOUR SPIRIT AS YOUR PHYSICAL STRENGTH GROWS, THEN YOU RISK THE DEATH OF YOUR SPIRIT IN THIS LIFE TIME AND IT MAY TAKE YOU LIFE TIMES TO REGAIN IT. Now before you put this book down and run as fast as possible from it, understand and hear the very next thing: YOU ARE PROBABLY ON THE ROAD TO THE DEATH OF YOUR SPIRIT IN THIS LIFE TIME WITHOUT THIS SYSTEM OR ANOTHER LIKE IT AND IT MAY TAKE YOU LIFE TIMES TO REGAIN IT.

If you are as morally weak as this world has created most people than you are probably saying "I'm damned if I do, I'm damned if I don't!" At the same time, you're asking why the hell did you ever pick up this book. I'll tell you. You picked it up because you wanted to learn about The Manifestations of Ra. You didn't really believe fulfilling such a wish came without consequences did you? If you truly did believe acquiring such true knowledge was so easy, then you did not understand that which you wished for and probably believe so many of the negative and pejorative lies told about ancient culture dedicated to God you know as ancient Egyptian.

I am quite sure that the most spiritually weak of you are cursing me. There is no need to curse me. All I offered was a choice. If you didn't know your spirit was dying in this world, you're either lying to yourself or you lack the knowledge that is contained in this book.

Before the self perceived spiritual amongst us scream about false Gods of Egypt there is no need for you to even bother. None of what can save you involves you changing religions. Just consider this a fine tuning of how you live your life. You can keep the God which you clutch in the middle

The Book Of Knowing The Manifestations of Ra *Again*

of the night and keeps you warm against the storm. Herein you will find a mostly a discussion of obvious truths which when put together create a systemic approach to optimizing your existence in the middle of the foulest time in human history.

Lastly and most importantly, this is no fire and brimstone speech; no attempt to guilt you into doing the right thing. I honestly could care very little about what happens to you. I want nothing from you. I am simply stating the truth as one of many caretakers of a part of this ancient culture and I have a responsibility to the ancestors to give you the truth in order so that you may make an informed decision based upon that truth and not the madness with which this society has chosen to portray Ancient Egyptian cultures.

As you can tell by now this is not simply a martial art book with techniques. It is, in few words, the most awesome internal energy management system and its spiritual component. You will see later how this is the truth and why it was kept a secret.

These warnings and this discussion may seem dramatic but it is this mystery system and its progeny which has served as the foundation for some of the greatest conspiracies against humankind from the Illuminati to the Nazi. They know who they are and could come to my doorstep and would drop dead. I fear them not. However, this does not change the fact that the manipulation of the lowest levels of Ra has killed many. This is why its symbols once held to be God's own are now seen as evil and to be feared instead of evil fearing it. The lowest levels of Ra will empower your impure spirit to achieve WHATEVER it will. And, as anyone knows, a powerful impure immature spirit will only abuse and use others around it. This is the cause of the problems of today's world. Knowingly or unknowingly strong immature spiritual children have taken control of the world and it is up to us to become spiritual adults and regain control of our home. Failure in this task means nothing less than the certain destruction of humanity. By the Great God AmenRa, let us become spiritual adults and let God reign upon this earth or die trying to become His warrior for Her Glory. "As upon earth -so in Heaven. Amen?" No, Amen- Ra!

The Book Of Knowing The Manifestations of Ra *Again*

ONE
The Great Stories

    If every Christian knew of Jesus' works, then every conversation a spiritual teacher had with a student could illuminate with quickness what was to be done in overcoming the spiritual issues confronting the student. Predating Christianity by a millennia, this was the purpose served by the great stories of Ra, Heru, and Ausar-the three most ever present aspects of the One God in the Pert Em Hru, the Egyptian bible, for lack of a better word..

    A necessary aside and word of clarification here. The Pert Em Hru was never called the Book of the Dead by those who entombed its passages with their dead or studied it while living in ancient Egypt. No, it was called by title, the Book of Becoming Awake which is what Pert Em Hru translates to. Here too, understand that it is meant becoming spiritually awake. In essence, the dead were buried with an instructional manual telling, reminding, exhorting them to remain awake so that they may make the passage to heaven. If you can visualize what would happen if this Christian culture decided to bury all the dead with a copy of the bible and 5000 years from now when there is no more Christianity someone dug up the graves, and

The Book Of Knowing The Manifestations of Ra *Again*

noted the bibles were in all the caskets, then decided that the bible should be called the book of the dead because all the dead had a copy; then you would know what happened to the culture of the Kamau, ancient Egypt, when the tomb raiders did their work. No, it was not a book of the dead but of the awake, the awakening of those who could become Hru, Heru!

Who was the God Heru? It was that aspect within the Kamau which choose to fight evil within and sometimes without so that peace and harmony could reign within and without. This aspect of God within was often interposed with Ra as Ra Heru or Herukhuti, and so many other formulations.

Let us speak for a moment about Gods for greater clarification because I realize that the greatest obstruction most of you will experience in accepting (note that I did not say converting to) any of the system which could save your lives and this world is your belief that the Kamitian culture was one which worshiped idols and many Gods. Understand that there was never ever, ever more than one God for the Kamau as well as any other non European religion just as Christianity does not have more than one God. You see man in his infinite limitations can and has conceptualized his Creator, but has always had the never ending need to explain Its role in the things of the world. This has lead him at differing times through out his history to give this Creator different names and attributes but yet It has remained singular and indivisible. No, not many gods with different names, but the One God with many different names--attributes--and so stories to explain those attributes or roles in nature. From Ti Kaui Li of the Taoist Immortals to the Hindu Shiva and the 101 names of Allah in Islam, there has ever been but One God . You see in their tongue, these names had meaning just as the Father means that He is Our Father...Consider that. No, I mean it--pause a moment and consider that. These names given any aspect of God were not just some made up name. Saying Maat in ancient Egypt was like saying in an instant "the Divine Love inside all of us for the humanity that our brother is willing to give to our sister without thought for a gift in return. To say Maat was to instantly encapsulate the Good Samaritan story, to retell the whole of Jesus' sacrifice for Humanity with one word. Now, do you see how I did not have to tell you what sacrifice and you did not even stop to ask what sacrifice? You live in this culture and accept that "God so loved the world and so gave his only begotten Son. And those who believe in him shall not die but have life ever lasting..." Had you lived thousands of years ago and you knew of Heru's great battle against his evil uncle Set, and you would not question someone telling you that for success you need to consult the oracle.

The Book Of Knowing The Manifestations of Ra *Again*

Now to understand Heru and the great battle with Set, you must understand the reason for the battle. The tale begins much like Genesis only historic moments before a fully populated Garden of Eden. God has created itself, the earth, and then populated the earth. There was no order amongst humanity. Without rule, man sought to fulfill only his most basic instincts usually at the expense of his sister and brother. Little more than savage death was the call, conflict-the toll, grief, and misery the toil. There was no harmony amongst a great many and humanity collected in groups only to the degree that it served the individuals. Out of this hard life rose Ausar. Ausar had come to understand the need to love God and to express God in every human action. He taught man to love each other and to care for one another in that love. This love once taught returned to Ausar in kingly fashion as he was given a throne to rule over the people whose lives he changed. Along with his wife Auset, he also taught man to cultivate the earth. Once achieved, Harmony reigned in Ausar's kingdom as each good soul cared for the other as peace lived within Ausar's touch. Filled with the love and compassion for all humanity Ausar knew that harmony had to reign beyond his kingdom's rolling hills of lavish cultivated lands. Understanding his responsibility, he set aside his kingly duties often to travel carrying the ways of peace and harmony to others, talking and showing, never forcing. In his absence, it was his wife Auset who ruled the kingdom.

There came a day when Ausar returned to the kingdom and there was a great celebration. His brother Set, who never lived Ausar's teachings, plotted to overthrow the good king. With the aide of the fiends of the Sebau, lowlifes of the highest order, Set tricked Ausar into a coffin which he presented the king. The original Set-up! Set then carried away Ausar and went on to hack Ausar into 14 pieces and placed his body parts in different spots across the earth. In great sorrow but determined, Auset left the kingdom and went in search of her mate. In her absence, Set seized rule and pronounced himself king of Ausar's Kingdom. With the aide of the Sebau, Set initiated a system of government based upon greed and force that was bereft of the divine love which Ausar had taught. God and man feared Set except for Auset's sister and later wife of Ra--HetHeru who lived in the clouds, and God's divine mouth piece and fountain of wisdom--Tehuti. With the aide of HetHeru, the goddess of joy, Auset found each piece of Ausar and while Ausar was still dead had his child. This child was Heru. And Heru would live down through the ages as Herucules or Hercules and eventually become Hero--those like Heru.

The great holder of Amen, son of Ausar, child of Auset, the

The Book Of Knowing The Manifestations of Ra *Again*

awesome grandson of Ra taught in the ways of war by Ausar after his birth waged either a three day or 200 year war against his father's brother Set, depending upon the version of the story. After a lengthy stalemate, Heru sought out Tehuti who was known as wisdom in order to overcome his uncle.

As Heru was the nephew of Set, Tehuti knew there could be no end in which Heru killed Set, for that would be barbaric and serve no other cause save vengeance. Tehuti instructed Heru to capture Set and bring him before the company of Gods. Heru did so either using Set's own trickery or brute force. Once before the company of Gods, Set bowed before them and conceded power to the company. To strike the balance which must ever reflect in the universe, Heru was given power over the light, Set power over the darkness in the human world. Forever more it would be up to humanity to choose the light of Ausar's Kingdom now ruled by and accessible only through Heru or choose Set's darkness devoid of the plentiful ness and breadth of human love under Heru's crown.

Of course, this is merely the archetypal story of good and evil. And if we apply our first lesson of understanding this spirituality, then by extension these characters are no more than, but much more than, aspects within us which we must empower to live our struggle for spiritual enlightenment and behavior on this planet. This great civilization was telling all who would listen that we must dig deep within ourselves and give birth without another's aide to the Heru within us all so that it may do battle with the Set within us so that a stalemate may be reached and then true victory had with Heru on the throne--in charge of our waking daily lives-- attempting to recreate Ausar's kingdom out of Set's darkness.

And what was Set's darkness? Why anything that was not Ausar's kingdom. Ausar's kingdom has many incarnations. Choose a word--hetep, nirvana, Christ's kingdom, B.F. Skinner's ideal community, Eden. It has been searched for and posited through out time. Anywhere where the needs of the many are ignored, greed pits man against man and war and the rumor of war abounds.

Yes, look around you Set is alive and well. Many starve in the midst of plenty and nuclear war is always on the brink. Welcome to hell and it is on earth. Now, you must choose to become Heru and seek to reestablish HIS kingdom on HER earth. No other goal is worthy. Any other goal is the great stalemate which is Set's victory. But how do you become Heru? And when will you know Ausar's kingdom? Lesson's for another moment....For now read on.

The Book Of Knowing The Manifestations of Ra *Again*

Assume that you have survived each battle with your own demons within, Set and his fiends of the Sebau, and were able to over come your dark emotions and loved your fellow man at every one of her turns; that you were able to hug your angry friend after it was over, that you were able to give the money to those who needed your money even though they cursed you, that you were able to....truly understand what it meant to live as God would upon the earth: Ausar, Christ, et al...and were able to actually live it..ACTUALLY LIVE IT.

And now what do you do? Within your own body flows the stuff of Ausar. Purified, you have nothing but peace and prosperity, friends and family because you give and so receive and are loved by all. Remember as Ausar you also fight Set, for was it not Ausar who taught his son Heru the ways of war? Many do not understand this about Ausar. They believe to become Ausar is to leave the fight. No, it is just the opposite. If you will not fight for your kingdom, when assailed or stolen, who else will? Perhaps one may....

Let us consider the great story of mighty Ra, self begetting and self begotten, the aged tireless one; Ra, the life, health, strength which breaks the back of the foul; back breaker of the wicked...Ra the Great Fiery One, the God of the Sun. Ra, who along with Amen or Amsu, and Ptah form the great triad of Annu a millennia before the story of Heru. The triad would merge into the great God AmenRa!

Now, today you understand that there is much darkness in the world and coming with the kind word which could change the world could get you hacked into pieces and spread the world over so Ausar's approach is difficult at best. However, the enemy is there all around you but it does not openly attack. Now there is time and need for your life force to be used by God for Its Divine Will upon the earth. An incredible honor, but a dangerous task. The story of Ra, the father of Ausar and Son of Nu, the primordial nothingness from which all things flowed--also called Amen, provides insight. You see it was said that daily Ra fought the great serpent Apep for reign over the sky as he lead souls to heaven from earth. At night, the two combatants rested and in the morning, the fight would renew again. And as Ra returned to Amen and slept Apep had a greater hold upon things of the earth. This story was a millennia old before Ausar's story held sway over the spirituality of the Kamitians. An epoch before Ausar and light and darkness are at each other's throat, eh? Be awake at day and do not sleep for evil will gain ascendance. Coincidence?

No, this is just the eternal metaphor for the fight of good over evil!

The Book Of Knowing The Manifestations of Ra *Again*

And the keys for our understanding are hidden in Ra's names: the double ax wielder, the double Heru--Herukhuti, life health, strength!--Ra's title seen very many places His name is---the Fiery One, Back Breaker. Got it? Still need a hint? What was Heru truly? Heru fought and He fought and he fought evil Set again and again. Heru was a warrior who became a spiritual king when evil was roped. So what was Ra if He was twice Heru--the fire that burns twice? He was the super warrior against evil! And that is what we must become if humanity is to survive.

Let us become the greatest spiritual warriors to ever walk the planet and lead souls to heaven upon earth....Ausar's kingdom. This is the point of this retelling of Knowing the Manifestations of Ra. The how lies between these pages.....

The Book Of Knowing The Manifestations of Ra *Again*

TWO
AMEN
The River of Life

It's going to take more than just some shoes to get you home, eh Dorothy? This should be clear by now.

What I mean is that if you are still with me, then it is pretty clear that spiritual strength and power-Amen and Ra, respectively, are clearly not just a wish away.

A story. One day, during the writing of this book, I'm at work where I am just a lowly cashier. No one respects me or regards me very highly, after all what black man with grey in his beard would be a cashier, but one to be lowly regarded. So much for the meek and the small inheriting anything, Eh? Well there is one group that regards me very highly, so much so that my best friend wants to call me king of the gypsies. Palm readers, tarot readers, crystal healers are always walking through my place of work getting jobs done. One such tarot reader and faith healer walks in the store. I feel her spiritual psychic attraction immediately. (This is not sexual). I put up my defenses and she constantly probes. The minute I'm distracted she's successful and gains

The Book Of Knowing The Manifestations of Ra *Again*

entrance. The next thing I know she's reading me.

"You should let me read you. I sense great powers, great gifts, I see things coming to you great wealth, prosperity..." she says intensely, even amazed. I look at her expressionless. Besides the fact that all who have ever read my destiny in the oracles saying the same thing in the past, I have by this time overcome being impressed by anything of the world, even my own destiny...(and that is the only way to be in the world and not of it--the key to all the keys)

She is amazed by all of this, my humility more so than what she saw. Most people would lose their world in hopes that what she had said would come and want for a map and details to the riches, then waited for them to come and fail to live the rest of their lives. I told her I knew all of this and started to talk to her about the Tarot being an inferior oracle...(again amazed that I knew she was a reader.)

"You should be proud of your gifts," she said.

"Then who would I be...." I answered. It was later in recounting the story that my mate told me I could be the great magnificent Oz.

Now I am not the foolish Oz and you are not the even more foolish Dorothy, however there are lessons here. You see you live in Oz and you are under a spell cast by the dark powers which rule this world-the real Oz. I say this in all seriousness. Dorothy was a fairy tale, was it not? No it wasn't. It was an adult story told to kids and there are many lessons to it.

Like Dorothy you are internally empty-eternally wanting for another place, time, thing to live away from what you know. Bored of life when life is all you need know. And the great OZ! Your doorway of imagination has led you to his kingdom where you are more a puppet than his flying monkey things. Daily you go to work for Oz, at night you sit in trance eyes glazed over and flip through each one of his conditioning television stations. To overcome boredom have sex, Oz tells you, while you buy new dish soap as you look at the lovely hands on the commercial. Or buy the car...house that all the beautiful people you either want to look sexy like or have. And then you sleep for two hours a night, of course you had to see the latest shows and talk to all the other enchanted(read under spell) people on Oz's phone before you got to bed. There in the most precious time you have, what do you do? Dream of being his flying monkey, buying his newest thing. Oh, the spell is deep. No spell you say? But it is and it is based upon the principles of the AmenRa Enlightenment so it is only in this system and its progeny in which the answers lie....

Now look at your one dollar US currency bill. What is the "Great

The Book Of Knowing The Manifestations of Ra *Again*

Seal?" It is a pyramid and an eye! The eye of Ra! Symbols manipulated, once meant for evil to fear, now to be feared by the Good Godly people for very few trust the US government. There is more than cooptation at work. And what the dollar bill, every bill say? "In God We Trust." This is a country which has always been based in the loosely termed Judeo-Christian faith. Well where's the cross on the dollar bill? Where's the Virgin Mary? Where are any of the Christian idols? I said it- a cross is an idol.(Just another part of Oz's plan, tell you that everyone else-with the truth to break his spell- worships idols and craven images, then gives you his to keep you in Oz.) No, the God trusted in is the system which gives you the power over this world!!!! You, land of Oz occupant must have the one-Christ- which will keep Oz burgeoning and satisfying the great Oz's will-no matter whether his name is Bush, Clinton, Goodnight, Hess or James Baker. "Rend unto Caesar what is Caesar's!" Is that a Christian motto meant to help foster harmony, help the Christian live in the world but be not of it? No! It is an attempt to keep you enslaved! Any tie with Set is his victory! He must be taken beyond the earth to the company of Gods and controlled! Hypnotized, cast under the spell, dare I say it- asleep, and you must become what?! Awake! Breathe in pure fresh air, drink the waters of life and cast out this foul demon you sleep with!

Ha, yes, indeed. you were asleep, But now you have found the magic shoes and I guess I'm the good witch of the West. Where does the Set? West-for those of us who don't know. What did Ra do when the sun went down--fought Set! As what? Amen! (Amsu or Atemu-Amen's other names.) Do you still doubt this to be the power? Doubt this as a way to serving in this endless war of good vs. evil? Then why have you dreamed of being Dorothy, or some other character in Oz since shortly before or after buying this book? And if you have been dreaming that you were Oz, you have serious work. For you are nothing despite all your wealth and worldly power and are under the spell so deep that your immortal soul is at stake and not even 5000 flying monkeys can bring you to His Love. You, above all must do what I ask next before everything else.

We must all let go of the things of the world! Say it to yourself again. I must let go of the things of the world! No need to click the heels together just cut up the credit card. Only buy what is necessary. This is Amen. The primordial waters from which all things flow. It is nothingness! And by contemplating nothing-ness in trance nightly then you will become a part of everything! Amen is the God of Nothing and Everything! Nightly you will go into a deep trance using the meditations discussed in this book and see yourself turning your back on things of the world until you are alone and

The Book Of Knowing The Manifestations of Ra *Again*

there is nothing but you in the night sky, then you will have no body, only your perceiving the sky, then no stars or light only darkness. It is here in these moments of trance that you will drink of the waters of life you will store them at the seat of the cobra and be fortified! You spiritual strength will start to rise. You will start to be able to tap into the waters of life at will during your Awaken state... This world will then start to hold no sway over you. You will come to understand that during sleep we all naturally rejuvenate at the waters of life. You will no longer sacrifice your drinking of the waters of life for the great Oz. Sleep and trance will be more important to you then selling the great Oz your life force for twelve to fifteen hours a day in exchange for his useless green paper. You will understand that you need sleep above all so that your spirit may fight the Oz! So that Ra will be strong in the morning to fight the Great Serpent! Victory over Set and his minions starts at night and occurs and night! The morning and day tasks are only the victory lap where souls are led across the battle field over the broken enemy. Understand?

    Good, then you also understand that if you do not battle him at night--dream and trance time is when your spirit is strongest and God within can express itself to your mind-than you can not even hope to lead on the battle field, for you will be picked off before engaging the enemy. You will lose the peace of your home to his Sebau, your life force will he suck with his fangs of green paper.

    A last word. Nurturing of Amen will empower all of the watery modalities of God within you. I don't want to be too complicated as that would be contrary to the intent of this book-re-giving the bomb in an easy fashion. Understand only that in this system, if you have to be soft and nurturing within an individual task Amen will help you. Many systems have different names for the varying grades of water and the combinations of the elements. This is the great yin yang, heat and water. The other combinations will naturally fall out in the shifting.

    Now understand Amen is also your greatest ally in overcoming the great physical power you will be working on in upping your Ra force. You see you must be able to control it and only want and need for nothing will. As you are nothing then you will have no emotional responses when you will not to. No anger. No fear. No depression. Nothing. No-thing. Then you can start to remember how it feels to be joyful when you want to.

    Are you angry and you need to stop the anger in order to avoid killing someone? Depressed and need to stop in order to become happy before you commit suicide? Stop, breathe, and remember how it felt to see

The Book Of Knowing The Manifestations of Ra *Again*

that blackness from atop the world in your nightly meditation. This will stop the emotion. Then return to the world and behave as you wish. Do as you will.(more on this later)The more you do this, the easier it will become and the quicker it will become until any emotion you want(will) is but a thought away. However, you must be rigorous and do it each time. Your spirit will become trained to go back and forth between what you know as reality and the waters of life, just as you can drive home from work almost with your eyes close...The method will be ingrained in your spirit. You will not have to think peace, but will(be)peace. You will bring back the ability to overcome what ails you, let alone all the power you need to do what ever you have to(will). Each time you do it you will be strengthening your spirit's power over the world. Heru! Heru will walk forward with you from your trip to the river Amen and help you establish Ausar's kingdom by defeating Set(emotional sickness).

See how you can deny jealousy to give to those in need now? See how you can deny depression now? See how you can deny your great sexual need for the woman with a jealous lover or the man in a relationship. See how you can deny any negative emotion or thing now?! No emotion means then that you merely need think of the emotion you want and it will be there. No depression think (read will) joy! No emotion also means you can then take a reading with the provided oracle and do as it states not what you want.

Sound simple eh? Read on and you will find in practice that it is more difficult than you imagine.

The Book Of Knowing The Manifestations of Ra *Again*

THREE
RA
The sun and two cobras versus a serpent

Herein lay the most secrets which have been stolen by the immature spirits which have mutilated a great spiritual system. Right now, you are reading this; you are ingesting it through the left side of your brain. Your breathing is slow and steady in all probability. Your blood is pumping slowly and evenly through your body as your heart pumps at its resting rate. You are at rest. If this material is foreign to you, then you may even be fighting boredom and staying alert, awake, despite all my efforts at mirth, levity, and creativity to keep the material fresh and interesting. On the other hand you may be at such a spiritual level that you can not help but continue to read at a quick pace wanting to get to the next word, chapter, the end because you know this all to be true and the thing for which you have lived every moment before this. Let us try an experiment to prove a point. Get up and do some exercise, just enough to get your heart pumping faster. Jumping jacks will do. If it is impractical to do exercise now, wait until when you can to finish the

The Book Of Knowing The Manifestations of Ra *Again*

chapter. Caution: do not over do it. We only want your heart to beat faster, your lungs to take in more air....

Welcome back. Now you should be reading this faster. The material should be easier to ingest. As your heart beats faster, your lungs take in more air, guess what you have become? Awake! Guess what makes your blood pump so? Yes your heart, but only partly. Yes, your brain, but only partly. Yes your life force but only mostly! You can have an almost dead brain and still be alive. And how many world leaders have weak hearts?(If I only had a heart...a brain...of course Oz has been on the planet long before the movie...) But let your life force leave you and your relatives will not need a doctor to tell them you are dying before they start to make the arrangements.

So now, in a crude way, we know that the life force, soul, spirit, etc, makes the blood pump faster. And what gave the life force more life? Or we should ask what gave the life force a greater hold over the waking state that our brain held sway over? Exercise...Exercise opened the door way to the spiritual world and let our spirits have greater domain over world. Purely simplistic, but true never the less. And what will we call this use or part of the life force that now courses through our bodies making it hot so that we sweat and our vision narrows and we are able to think sharply and clearly and we feel as if we could have sex for hours and run forever and....

Ra! Chi! Kundalini! Qi! Yang! Name a spiritual discipline which seeks to harness the life force and we can find its counterpart.

Now you must trust me for an ancient spiritual fact. An awakened life force is a treacherous thing. A life force can be awakened with out reaching its maximum ability to control our actions and merely empower our bodies to do things beyond the ability of most mortals. A completely enlivened life force is the stuff of spiritual dreams, the state for which all spiritual quests reach. Once completely awake the life force flowing through you and me can change the world and do miracles. It is nothing less than God living in the world through or in your vehicle. It was codified by the Kamau as Ra, Heru, or Ausar.

Let us retrace our steps and apply the great stories for a minute. You exercise and breathe using the meditation techniques of the following chapters and what happens? You awaken Heru who is able to see the world around you and who is now strong enough within you to whisper, "My(your) world is in a shambles. There is naught but decadence all round and Set and childish emotions of jealousy, envy, deceit and all the rest of his foul depravity rule my(Our) Father's kingdom.. My heart is heavy. I pick up my sword and will hack out the Father's kingdom." Slowly Heru fights wins and

The Book Of Knowing The Manifestations of Ra *Again*

Ausar becomes ruler of your world as Set is pushed back. Now you know God and can share, you can give for you know there is no separate individual, you can control your temper, you are not jealous. You can in essence commit miracles. No need for the obvious ones, healing of others, etc, though they are possible; for would it not be a miracle to simply be able to overcome all the emotional compulsion that flashes into your awareness!

Now. to the next level. Set is firmly bound and gagged within your awareness. He has been placed deep down beneath your spirit firmly under Ausar and you are experiencing fruits of His kingdom in your life. Because you share, everyone shares with you. Because you are unemotional most of the time, then nothing but balance is in your life. No longer a resident of Oz, you look upon the envy, the other passions, and pure foolishness of emerald city and smile knowing it to be only a foolish dream. Then from within one day, you hear it. Small, at first. "My child will you sit by and let them that know me not destroy me, for there is only me in the world?" Then you know you must fight them, but there are so many and much to be done. And you know that the open war will be hopeless for Set is thick in Oz and all will think you mad. (After all only lunatics speak to God in a Godless society. And surely you must be mad, if great wealth gained by denying the poor is wrong, if destroying the only home we have with pollution is crazy, if selling people death(fast foods--preservatives) for more wealth by a few is sick) Still you are God's child. You know it clearly, brighter than any sun in the sky it burns you--you are God's child. And he has called you to His war for Her glory! What do you do? You train. And you train like any soldier would. Heru beats strong within and Ausar's kingdom is without in your immediate grasp. You now pick up Ra's ax and His ways to battle this serpent all round for the crossing of souls over to His glory in this world. Ra, Heru, Ausar...these are the glories of a purified spirit in this world.

But what of the world in which a spirit just coming to life is cut short in its growth? Look around you, you are living in it. This is why this system has been used by the plots against humankind. You don't have to consider such extremes as the Nazi or even the Illuminati. Think of how exercise is used to fulfill the lower passions. Any newsstand will do: work out to work harder at your desk (in Oz!) This is behind the after noon work-out that has swept corporate America. Don't **fall asleep** at your desk after lunch by working out at lunch. You work harder for the bondage of America to money used for what? To create more money not love....The list is endless. Ever tried to work up the courage to do something you knew you should not have done?

The Book Of Knowing The Manifestations of Ra *Again*

What did you do? Odds are you breathed deeply! And you may have even breathed deeply quickly! And you can bet that the members of the Illuminati that run this world do not have coke running through their veins, but pure life giving water!

So now the preamble done, let us talk about creating the temple of God within and raising the Ra force to control it. Stick with it Dorothy and I promise you that you will not have to click your heels nor be told. You will know that you are dreaming. What? You don't like the analogy. Well then you will suddenly see the numbers of the Matrix and Neo will come looking for you and everyone else will wake up. There will be no more Matrix!(didn't know that I knew about those dreams. Some just need a grown up Hollywood movie, that's all and the Matrix will do.)

First we must work out, four to five days a week, both aerobically and anaerobic ally. We have seen the need for testosterone and weightlifting will do. The west has stated all the benefits of weightlifting on testosterone and we have looked at the need for testosterone before. Remember Life!Health!Strength! Both men and women should lift.

Eat correctly. The temple can not be strong without a firm foundation! Remember to drink water, the store house of life! All attempts should be made to move toward a vegan diet.

Spend as little time in the Matrix, in Oz, in this system participating in it. So much energy is lost chasing dreams of this system---wealth, promotion, accolades--- you worry your life long during the day and do not leave it at work but bring it home, where you worry more in front of their Matrix, Ozian, amplifiers the TV. and radio. Turn it all off. (To be sure one still needs to participate in this system but a balance in favor of the spiritual must be struck.)

Have sex, inorgasmic sex and plenty of it. More on this later.

Meditate during the waking day by keeping your breath at all times in the seat of the cobra as you maintain upright posture. Remember the glyph of the front cover the sun is the torso, the snakes your lower stomach. This will keep your Ra force high, you will remain awake. And when challenged, your life force Ra will be in abundance just a breath away to forcefully exert itself in your world against Set or Apep. The sun and two cobras against the serpent. Breathe deeply into your sun and cobras each time you have an emotional urge--smoking death, killing friendship, anger etc. Keeping focused on this it will be easier to call the Ra disk to respond to your will when dealing with enemies. The visualization is easy- simply see the Ra disk going out from you to dispose of your enemies. It will be clear. Remember

The Book Of Knowing The Manifestations of Ra *Again*

this is God working not you. And there must have been an oracle reading first or it will boomerang on you.

Stretch. It is not necessary to take yoga, if it is impracticable. Simply stretch every muscle in the body. Morning and night(be mindful at night not to stretch overly or even vigorously; for you will find it difficult to sleep as you will awaken the life force). The body is made of energy meridians which can be blocked and will block your spirit's road to and from the waters of life. A blocked energy can not serve. You don't want such a simple thing as being tight to stop the most powerful thing in your universe. Do you?

And that's almost it. So if it was as easy as that then why are not Olympian athletes great spiritual warriors, if they love God? Two things. This is not only it, exercise is just a piece of the pyramid. And who says they are not....

The quest deepens and all becomes clearer before the balanced scales of Ra's justice in the following pages....

The Book Of Knowing The Manifestations of Ra *Again*

FOUR
MAAT
Mistress of the Gods and Daughter of Ra:
The scales of justice
From Maa Kheru to the Extended Relationship
From the flint of Magic to the very real power of Love
From friendship to participation in the human race
From the heaviest feather in the Universe to the truth in great wealth

    Here, in these pages relating to the great aspect of God known as Maat is the difference between the professional athlete and God's spiritual warrior. A word of repetition: If, by now, you tire of the spiritual warrior image or you find it offensive, then please understand that this is the spiritual system behind a martial art/health system. The Useru, the initiate, in this system is at war for his very soul and the adept, the Sesh, is at war for the souls of the Useru in touch with him. By its very terms, "martial," we are discussing war. As for the potential offensiveness caused by a disdain for the war created in God's name in the past, this is neither the intent nor purpose of this image. No Jihad (holy war) should be waged or has ever been waged

The Book Of Knowing The Manifestations of Ra *Again*

in the name of Ra. Those wars were waged by foolish men for the sake of foolishness. In the year 2000 and then more, we must be spiritually mature enough to say that war is anti-human and merely a tool of Set and Apep and the fiends of the Sebau which sows Set-apartness and pain and toil and trouble when union and unity should be the goal of the entire planet.

No, the war raged here in AmenRa Enlightenment is a true spiritual war on planes unseen by the naked eye or the spiritually immature which involves the Useru and the Sesh as they use their internal spiritual and physical health against all that that is unholy (against the whole-no?)

That said let us speak of Maat, mistress of the Gods and Daughter of Ra. What can I say about Maat which has not yet been said by so many current scholars both spiritual and secular? Perhaps nothing, however perhaps I can help you understand its practice in daily life so that what seems mystical is merely the mundane, common place.

In Maat, the Kamau codified their entire culture as they had never done under any one God, except perhaps in Ra. However, in Ra they had also placed their understanding of the creation of the universe and overcoming of evil. You see Maat was their cultural Aesthetic, way of seeing the world and how one would fit in the world spiritually. To be sure, this was demonstrated in what is known as the 42 admonitions of Maat or the negative confessions.

It was Maat's mate, the aspect known as God's Divine wisdom, Tehuti who revealed to humanity God's divine plan (yes, just as Tehuti had revealed God's plan to Heru so that Heru could overcome Set) during deep trance or through the use of oracles as the one provided in the next book of this work. It was also Tehuti who presided over the weighing of the heart ceremony, over which Maat also presided. Everyone has seen this scene if they have ever looked at Egyptian "art." The dual Maati stand over the heart of the deceased as it is weighed against a feather while Tehuti and Sebek look on. Tehuti is revealing fate and Maat is weighing the heart against her feather. (They were saying that love and wisdom were inextricably linked.) The heart which is physically heavier by any account than any feather balances the scale because it has remained light while on earth. And the secret here is that only a heart willed to be light can be...

To understand more, you must understand the Kamau's moral code. It was simple: One must act peacefully in harmony with everyone else (the whole). At peace is what the feather means. The light heart is the heart at peace, no? What happens when one is angry? The heart becomes heavy, no? The heart under stress is heavy. No? Understand that any action which

The Book Of Knowing The Manifestations of Ra *Again*

makes the heart beat harder is usually one in which the heart is heavy.

And what is harmony? Now, there is a subject of a volume of books. But for our purposes let us say that it is merely the state where the needs of the many are met by all, where everything fits where it should. Sharing to meet another's need, no? And it is sharing with out causing unnecessary dispute. (Sometimes dispute is necessary, just as denying another's needs despite being able to fulfill them are sometimes necessary for whatever reason).

Now when Ausar taught all to give to all to help the collective feed and house itself (read meet the most basic human needs), he taught Maat. Right? Not only did he do so but he must have done so with a light heart, a heart not feeling any emotional constraint. For if Ausar felt any emotional constraint, heaviness while doing this Maat work, he would not have been able to do it for long or for the great many he did, let alone travel the world teaching it. Doubt the heart was light? Well how long can the heavy heart evidencing duress last? How long before your heart feels as if it will bust when it is assailed by the emotions which you allow it to feel?

The light heart is what then? Happy! Happiest in all the world as it does Maat. Giving and sharing, forgiving (... "as we forgive those who trespass against us," No?) And most of all living...And if your heart becomes heavy then perhaps you should reconsider your reason for doing Maat.

The only reason that Maat should ever be done is because of recognition of the oneness of all life. Say it after me: heavenly MotherFather, that which I do for another, I do for you and I only do for myself. You see there is but one Spirit in the entire universe flowing through all of us. Our spiritual immaturity makes us believe in our own Set-apartness. But when we come to that moment when we are actually committing acts of selfless ness dictated by the understanding of the oneness of the human spirit, then the world truly opens up and we are magical beings with the power to move this world this way or that! Who else would God want to give the power to than someone who has come to understand he is his brother's keeper because he is his brother?

Yes, this is divine love, a love bereft of the baggage of age, sex, and color. Over the years, I have thought of many ways to explain it to the uninitiated. Many have been used, but I always remember the first time I tried to put it into words. I had just started on the path of the Tao. And my teacher was doing work with me to overcome the rage of my heart, the lack of the truly divine love. Suddenly, I felt the great need to call every friend whom I had seriously hurt emotionally and apologize. While this was

The Book Of Knowing The Manifestations of Ra *Again*

happening, I tried to explain what it to my friends and the best analogy I had was a parent's love to a child. Now with my understanding of Maat the analogy is only improved.(I did not know it then, but becoming open to the universe by meditation techniques given to me by my teacher, I was embarking on what is called a truth giving ritual practiced by Kamitic spiritualist) Now a parent will endeavor to meet the child's every need. The child's need for food, clothing, companionship, and spiritual, mental, and physical development will be recognized and met at any given point by a parent.

What you must understand that this the same relationship spiritual adults have for other spirits in the universe. You may think that the relationship is different--parents are responsible for children. No, it's just the same. When you understand and are truly living Maat, then you know that everyone is your responsibility as you are theirs, we are but links in the chain of life; individuated only by our own thought, not spirit. You will know when you have come to truly understand Maat, when there is nothing that you would not do for another when those oracles tell you to do so. You will sacrifice your time, energy, resources--your very self if called upon, for this is God's chain and another link calls for it. Should that link break because of your failure to aide it when it was under stress, then you loose your tangible connection with God...And Oh it will be tangible...

You see when you have done enough Maat--volunteer your services in your community, forgiving the world; given truth to others, healing your heart....becoming a part of this human race, then you will be given quite literally the power to move the mountains. You will be Maa Kheru, Maat will tell you so and no earthly force will stop you because Divine Love will answer your every call for aide.

Now what does it mean to be Maa Kheru? I have heard or seen it discussed many different ways. Let us say it is merely the point one comes to in their spiritual development where one has decided and knows that all are truly one spirit and every action one takes is in recognition of that fact. You are now the living embodiment of Divine Love. As the living embodiment of Divine Love, you are now given great powers by God. What you see comes true. What you want you are given and only because what you are given will be shared.

Understand that the Pert Em Heru discusses the deceased desiring himself be pronounced Maa Kheru at the appointed time. We know by now that the appointed time *is while on earth not after death*. Right? *Right*.

Let us understand something please. And no matter what I say do

The Book Of Knowing The Manifestations of Ra *Again*

not ignore this truth and don't argue with it. Hear it out then let all your worldly experience confuse you.

You will be given great powers by God, but these powers will be limited to the degree you are willing to work with the entire human race. You see you can recognize one spirit, but still be held back by the wrongs done to you and your kind by one kind or another. I'm speaking of racism or any other ill. Now is the moment that you must understand Divine Love means Divine Forgiveness. And this means you working on behalf of another or a member of another's group which may have done you wrong. Yes, slavery existed, but forgive. The Nazi killed, but forgive. Punishment? Well that is a reading to be done using oracles. There is greater growth for the vast majority in working with and loving all.

Please, before you start with the racial superiority and your righteous indignation and greater claim to an African religion because of your blackness. This is a religion hoping to unify all as it was originally meant to. These are not my desires but oracle commandments.

Once we can love our greatest perceived enemy, then a great liberation occurs to the life force and the powers it experiences are magnified almost exponentially. Refuse to forgive and love and you are merely limiting your powers, your gift, and your access to the human race. If you chose only to work with your clan, only with your race, only with your family, then you will be understood; for the spiritually mature realize that such a level of Divine Love takes great strength of heart and spirit; hence the need to strengthen the life force using A Ra.

Now about your question. If what you say in defense of all of your separatist actions: I can't forgive, "purple" people will kill me if...but don't you know what they did..." which ignore the host of ills perpetuated by your own kind unto you and yours; for until there is growth, all people copy Set's blueprint of pain and disunity; I say to you do you believe that God would give you All The Power, if you could not love ALL of His Creations on Her earth?

Sure now maybe you can do a miracle or two, but how long did that take to get there...and how in control of it are you, and what more do you want to do...for a percentage of Her world?

Look take your time...accept....and then live. I am not a man who has not been there....This is a very difficult level to achieve, that is why you need strength, physical as well as spiritual. And because you are sacrificing, stay close to oracle readings. You can not serve even yourself if you give up your world, your dignity...

The Book Of Knowing The Manifestations of Ra *Again*

All of that said about your dignity you can still serve the world. You see you will spend so much time in your nightly Amen meditations that you will slowly break the bonds of spiritual separation and become part of all. You will truly care about what happens to your fellow being. You will care whether they are loved, have clothing food or shelter.

As this power of Divine Love makes itself felt in your world be you male or female spiritual adult, then your thoughts will turn to the family as either a natural spiritual growth or a very difficult spiritual undertaking brought to you by the more spiritual advanced. Now this is not meant to be an advocate piece persuading you of the rightness of the extended spiritual union as a community vehicle; for this world is a selfish one and you have been raised in a very selfish way and the Extended Spiritual Relationship is an act of selflessness for the good of the many. And any one who has ever been to a religious gathering knows there are more women than there are men attempting to live spiritual lives in this world, for a myriad of reasons not really suitable for a discussion here.

Let us first define what the Extended Spiritual Relationship is first by stating what it is not. It is not polygamy. Polygamy, the marriage of more than one woman to a man, is illegal in America for so many reasons, too numerous to name here. The Extended Spiritual Relationship is intended for circumstances in which two married or one unmarried male and one or more female consenting adults agree to help each other and their children with their spiritual, physical, and mental needs. This is no multiple wife marriage under western law so there is no violation of law. This is not marriage. Those involved in Extended Spiritual Relationships do not hold themselves out as married nor do they intend for themselves to be married. Their intention is only to be responsible for their actions with another adult by taking care of spiritual and worldly responsibilities incurred in that relationship. Millionaires, athletes, entertainers and everyone else, take care of the relationships you so easily create and even more easily toss aside to the detriment of your growth and the health and welfare of everyone else involved! And if this isn't your life or you can not see the functionality or moral rightness of this, then mind your business. No, truly, tend to your closed minded business, and watch the world go by.

In AmenRa Enlightenment, the consorts can come out of the closet. Indeed, there need not ever be a closet for the consort to step into. What a world would it be when rich and powerful men could claim allegiance to their illegitimate child, their so called illegal woman they took care of for year upon year. Look around, I'm sure you could name several. Is this not a world

The Book Of Knowing The Manifestations of Ra *Again*

now where so much occurs that would argue for the Extended Spiritual Relationship? Are not these women and children already a part of these relationships, in some way, whether known or unknown by both the man and woman already in the relationship? Is not the man already meeting the needs of consorts? Is his recognized woman not already sacrificing her time and energy to a woman and child(ren) —whether she knows it or not?

I have done much work with many regarding this act and to a man or woman the discussion is the same. A woman wants her own man for her own sake and will be self righteous in her selfishness, even while recognizing the truth of the matter. "I know my sister needs. An Extended Spiritual Relationship is Maat, but not everyone is meant to practice it in their life time." (Meaning not me and my man.) Know this. That the force of Maat is so strong, especially within those that are practicing AmenRa and even more so within those practicing A Ra, that if you maintain this selfishness, you, not others will be left without that mate you did not want to share with the world eventually. Disbelieve because your "love" is so strong? Ask yourself this, "would God sacrifice the momentary pain of one for the Divine Love of the many?" Does not your sister need a companionship, protection, as well all the other adult physical and spiritual needs?

The answer is a resounding yes! If you want a mate for yourself alone than you shall have such, but do not hope to have such a relationship with one who is trying to live his life spiritually for His God upon Her earth, no matter how much you seek recourse and comfort in spiritually immature adults who are accorded spiritual respect in this world. There is no need to tell anyone practicing Maat what the so called spiritual author says about "the meantime" waiting for your own, no need to tell him about how crazy your girlfriends say he is, for they are still asleep in Oz.

And let us speak truth about relationships in Oz for a moment. There is no Divine Love to be had in the world so all are out to meet their own needs. Let us be "real" for a moment. In Oz a man is not a man unless he has at least two women. Right? A man is a prize sought by women with needs whether he is married or not, has a steady woman or not. (How many times have we heard, "I won't hurt her, I just need..") And how much creepin' sneakin' cheatin' is part and parcel of a culture where the presidents are the greatest illygamist there are. And if you are single, you are not above reproach. What is dating but illygamy? A man who is dating is looking to have sex with any one he dates. True? While a woman may or may not have sex with her dates. True. Well, let's be real again. Due to the nature of testosterone and other hormones created by the endocrine system, a man

The Book Of Knowing The Manifestations of Ra *Again*

dating told, "no" by a woman will find another to have sex with, even if he continues to date the non responsive female. Thereby meeting some of the needs of all the women he is in contact with. Is that not a form of union? Yes, its illygamy. A man should never have sex with a woman if he is not considering her for a serious relationship. It is dangerous physically and spiritually to both human beings. They are risking physical safety-diseases and harm, and objectifying each other.

Yes, the men are no better. Most men don't have the spiritual strength nor desire to be responsible for more than one woman, but they will have sex with another in a heart beat. Why be responsible for your actions with another when you can just have fun. He doesn't need the financial, spiritual, and physical responsibility. He just wants to take what he wants and will leave.

There are so many arguments that our "good" sisters under the spell can come up with. What about the dangerous diseases which having all those women bring. This assumes that any member of the relationship has these problems. But let's go even further; let's talk about the dangerous diseases which exist out side a marriage. Let me illustrate with a story.

During a time, a particular woman would come to my counter often. She was compelled by the spiritual forces attempting to save her to discuss her life with me. We begin a discussion about Extended Relationships. She says that I'm out of my mind of course, and that in a relationship people must be equally yoked. She questions why others who come to see me do as I ask them to and ignores my answer to her question--because I know the outcomes of things using oracles and that oracles keep our spirits and temples(bodies) safe in this cruel world. "I got my Jesus." She responds and despite my protestations--as mandated by oracle readings--decides to do what she pleases rather than listen to me. Months later, depressed, she returned to my counter with a drunkard who had infected her with a disease which may eventually kill her (unless she finds the divine power within and heals herself--a long bet since she would have to leave Jesus Oz to do so.)

This sad story illustrates a point. Dating is dangerous. (Not to mention life decisions) the Extended Relationship keeps the members safe while meeting their needs. There is another added degree of safety in the Extended Relationships of the AmenRa spiritualist. No consort would ever be taken on without a reading using high oracles which would keep the reader safe. No diseased individual would ever be allowed to be a member in the Relationship. Remember you do not forfeit your life to do Maat. A reading using just about any oracle would have kept this woman safe. But

The Book Of Knowing The Manifestations of Ra *Again*

don't just stop there. How much pain and trouble would be avoided by a Maat perspective in relationships. How much date rape avoided? How much bitter woman beating, psychological punishment, and a whole host of ills? No, don't tell me of the madness of Extended Relationships, let us speak of the madness of monogamy in this world now. Where would the marriage success rate be in this country, if this were practiced? But no, we want the illusion of functionality of exclusive monogamy with the practicality of disaster. I even had one women tell me she knows her man sees other women, but she's in love and just as long as she doesn't know them and never has to see them(This is a common belief by the way.) Wouldn't a sane position be to want to know who you are sharing this life with? But things are not sane in Oz, now are they? Presidents and the rich power brokers with multiple consorts trotted openly before the public innocuously and in sex scandals, but the poor are left to confuse each other trying to meet their needs and Extended Relationships that would do so are derided, belittled, cursed and more.

Finally, let us deal with the truth about truth. Many women want to say that Extended Relationships can't be practiced by a man at the center of the union who is not rich. Indeed many women won't join such a relationship if others involved are not rich. Should we call this woman a whore-- pimping herself? It certainly sounds that way does it not? Well these rules are set up in such a way for a reason having much more to do with the people in communities in which it is practiced than with Divine Love. But any true understanding of Maat deals with the fact that it is about sharing the resources to meet the needs of the many. Many adults mean many resources regardless of the man at the center. Sure, every man wants to take care of every woman, but spiritual growth at times does not allow it. (Remember you must let go of the things of the world for a moment in order to grow)

That is the true love of Extended Relationships —giving for then you shall receive. You see practicing of Divine Love guarantees great wealth, you share, and the universe will share with you. Male or female, when it is your time you receive almost more wealth than you can handle. These women waiting for the rich man to come along will wait until their hair is long and grey because of their selfishness (remember their response was about them, not about the needs of the whole.) Maat will not answer their prayers in a million years unless and until they change them.

Let us understand that in AmenRa Enlightenment, Extended Relationships are practiced according to the spiritual strength of the man at the center. His strength exhibited by his humane treatment of all around him,

The Book Of Knowing The Manifestations of Ra *Again*

his leadership in his community, his ability to exude spiritual strength and power and willingness to help others grow will be the determining factors concerning Extended Relationships. Let those who wish to pimp themselves worry about the amount of Oz's green paper in his Ozian bank account. We will assume that the spiritual strength will create the wisdom of using birth control methods until a child with new consorts can be afforded.

Finally, you know that following Divine Love and Law will keep you spiritually protected in this world no?(as evidenced by oracle readings—the oracle gives you truth, Divine Law). However, one word. Following the law means protection and wealth but it can not protect you from bad choices. Understand? Suppose the oracle indicates you should not take a trip, you do (bad choice betting against God's instructions) and the plane crashes. You walk away with many broken bones, brain damage etc, but everyone else dies, this, is your divine protection. But you will be in pain the rest of your life and half the person you once were. No. Do not depend upon doing good to protect you. You must make wise decisions with the aide of the oracles like the one offered in volume two of this work. The AmenRa Oracle.

The Book Of Knowing The Manifestations of Ra *Again*

FIVE
Hathor the goddess of Love
HetHeru, wife of Ra
Both the same and closest to the thing that moves you

Let us deal with the force of HetHeru. The thing that moves you. When I say that it is the thing that moves you, I mean that the spiritually immature are motivated by the things which they believe cause them pleasure. Don't believe me? I dare you to seek out what you do in your life and understand why you do a thing. I would be willing to bet that to a large degree you do things which lead in some way to some pleasure. HetHeru is standing there smiling, waiting at the end of some long, or short, spiritual endeavor just to teach you about real joy, real pleasure and what you learn may not always be what you wanted to learn. Ah HetHeru, tricky as she is beautiful, no?

She is the force in nature which drives the spiritually immature to a large degree. She is the aspect of God which we relate to pleasure, sensuality, sex, superficial happiness, just the plain old good time thing. Ancient secret: if your body and spirit connection is ecstatic than what ever you see will

The Book Of Knowing The Manifestations of Ra *Again*

impress itself upon your spirit. Your spirit will be conditioned to obtain it. (because it will associate that thing with ecstasy). So obviously you see why sexual items are used to sell things which have nothing to do with sex. The sexy models sitting on cars etc. As a result then you see that you should visualize things which you wish to obtain during ecstasy--this secret is shared by many religions which understand HetHeru in this way. For maturity sake let us simply say that during prolonged pleasure we should visualize that which is good for our lives. Once we are adept at using oracles we should ask God if we should visualize those things.

WARNING: This type of visualization is very dangerous, more so than you believe. A simple illustration: Let's say you want a man or woman, whether it is out of lust or some misguided understanding of love. You obtain the desired relationship with him or her. She/he then turns out to be a mass murderer. Far fetched you say?

Another story. A woman of wealth whom I had seen come to my store quite often came to the counter one night crying. She was there to receive a fax from her bank. Her boyfriend whom she loved dearly, or so she believed, had stolen vast sums of money from her investment and savings portfolio. She launched into this story about how much he had told her he loved her and how she wanted him etc. Trust that she had seen a successful relationship with this man many times when she should have been running full speed in the opposite direction. Perhaps an oracle reading could have saved her, perhaps not; for it could only have saved her had she followed the oracle's counsel-something the spiritually immature are not ready to do often; for it usually calls for one to be beyond emotions which the inquirer is in the grips of.

Let us assume that you have the oracle's permission to use your very real HetHeru powers in a given situation. During sex you visualize the achievement of the height of passion with your intended. When you see your intended outside of the passionate moments you breathe, drop the breathing into the seat of the cobra and see the intended at the heights of passion, and feel the physiological change come over you, a slight erection or mild lubrication. As that energy is transferred from you to them they too will feel it and whether they know it or not they will believe the thoughts, feelings etc to originate within themselves. Magic you say? How about plain old science. What you will be mastering is the secretion of hormones(yes, pheromones) to achieve your end. But your success depends upon many things. Firstly, your spirit must be strong. If you do not have a strong spirit then you will not have the strength to affect another's' spirit. A strong spirit is only created

The Book Of Knowing The Manifestations of Ra *Again*

through the spiritual practices of this book and others like it. Also, you must have spent much time in the spontaneous secretion of hormones and to do so your spirit must flow uninhibited. In other words you must be comfortable with being uninhibited. I am talking about being able to shift to a great level of arousal in mere seconds. You must spend time practicing this. It will help you greatly with meditation work as well as freeing your life force. Remember, I said that a high sex drive is companion to a high life force? No, I am not telling you to become a sexual deviant. I am telling you within the boundaries which we have discussed you must move freely with but a moment's thought. Lastly if you are a practitioner of A Ra or the AmenRa Enlightenment use of this power must be the will of God because your spirit will be so strong that you would probably be working these powers on the spiritually immature and you would be very spiritually responsible for the certain damage that will occur to them, if you use your spirit with out a reading. Yes, as you have guessed this method can work, because to a certain degree it is little more than chemistry, even without great spiritual ability. Yes, it is another reason why it has been kept part of the mystery in the mystery system.

Why such detail? Because the use of HetHeru goes beyond an intended, no matter how nice a lead in it was. You can use her power to obtain wealth when needed, to diffuse arguments, stop conflict, to create incredible art, and the list is endless. Know that the one of the highest uses of her power is to cool the Ra force she is nurtured by. Applying this to the world it means that the HetHeru force within the AmenRa Enlightenment practitioners can be an aide in stopping war. It can be used to stop it in a gentle way or in the forceful way. Again I remind you that it was HetHeru along with the eye of Ra who was sent out against the enemies of Ra. This is merely the metaphor of her the great strength spiritual sex may generate then how it may be used. The method is always the same. when I am in need of using her power I feel my attractiveness (not others attracted to me--there is a difference) I feel my happiness and more.

Another story so that you do not misunderstand and so misuse the powers which I am revealing to you. A woman was brought to me at my store by another woman whom I had helped overcome her sexual enslavement to men. This second woman had lost her job a while before she came to see me. She was depressed and broke, she was at her wit's end with another interview lined up soon, despite failing to get a job from all the other interviews she had had previously. I instantly did a reading on giving her the secrets above. She was a beautiful woman with a high life force repressed

The Book Of Knowing The Manifestations of Ra *Again*

beneath her Christianity, needing hours of prolonged sexual experience daily. After working past her repression and her amazement over how I knew all of this, I told her to go into the interview with her sex drive at its highest by refraining from activity and feel her attraction, and know that the interviewer would be seeing her this way. And that she would get the job. Well she got not one, but two jobs and was amazed. However in debriefing her, I found out that she had gone too far. Her imagination went to sexual experiences with the interviewers! What this got her into is the stuff of whole other books!! And of course because she had become successful, she could not hear any of the warnings I gave her, nor did she remember them when I first told her what to do. What had been most important was overcoming her at times near suicidal depression and an initiation into the strength of her spirit to work in the world which could lead to a savior of this incarnation to do the spiritual work she was meant to do. When last I saw her she didn't want to hear what I had to say. Currently it is the undeveloped spirit with the spiritual atom bomb. Do you need a road map to see the destination?

But enough of ends for the moment. Let us speak of roads to the end, and the destination we want to cultivate. Remember we are cultivating this great awsome aspect of God within us for a reason. That reason is not clear to you because your endeavors using it has always wound up in a scant moment worth of contractions in your genitalia. But if you learn to cultivate it correctly not only will you have great pleasure but great strength. The strength to stop conflict, even by turning the conflict into peaceful disagreements, create beauty, and the strength t—end war--remember it was Ra's eye and Hathor who were sent out to kill the enemies of Ra!

Placing demands upon your endocrine system with no release leads to a build up of hormones with no release. Without being too scientific let us just say that not only well known things produced like testosterone and estrogen and androgen and the like, but also growth hormone--which you will come to realize is responsible for all of the factors in the human body which make it look and feel young--rejuvenated! (the fountain of youth!!) Supplement healthy living--eat right, sleep nights—in orgasmic sex with the judicious use of the correct herbs, remove stress from your life--using the Amen techniques-- then you will not have to tell everyone about the fountain of youth you have found or your great strength, for they will see it long before you say two words.

In orgasmic sex is easy to say much harder to practice. Males must practice withdrawal and mastery of the penis and perineum muscle. Stop in the middle of arousal and breathe the sexual energy up into the seat of the

The Book Of Knowing The Manifestations of Ra *Again*

cobra and return to sex several times. When orgasm can no longer be put off then the male must grip the base of the penis holding down the vans deferens--the middle vein of the penis and severely squeeze the anus--the anus should be slammed shut all day and the male anus should never allow anything inward. Slowly over time, if he is persistent the male will master the technique of experiencing the convulsions of orgasm without dropping any sperm by simply squeezing(using muscle control only) the perineum, prostate, and anus region. Withdrawal during intercourse without orgasm which is immediately followed by meditation in the seat of the cobra will lead to intense internal orgasm which will greatly enliven and strengthen the life force.

    To enhance male sexual strength and therefore life force a man should buy himself a penis ring and even a pump. An erection should be attained while using these devices then the penis and perineum should be rubbed with hot herbal lotion such as Bengay. (Careful of the application- put a very thin film on at first for it will burn unlike anything you know. But with consistent use the tolerance built up will allow quite a pasting.) This practice draws massive amounts of blood and life force to the area stimulating many of the great life force channels with in a man. Side effects of this work results in great testosterone and growth hormone levels, and an erection as strong as an arm with great huge veins. Men please be gentle with all your new found strength--the ability to have hours of sex- and continue Amen work so that you do not use the strength you have wished for all your lives in pursuits which will ruin your spiritual life.

    To enhance female sexuality is vastly simple, yet complex. Women should buy themselves what the sexual spiritual literature calls the golden egg. The device is inserted with in the vagina and simple contractions are done. This work can be aided by application of hot herbal paste upon the perineum complex as well as clitoris, the hood and major lips. (Most women will find that a peppermint paste or candy applied directly is more than hot enough) Women will also find great pleasure and strength derived from in orgasmic sex as described above using the seat of the cobra meditation. A note: a woman can have orgasm after long periods of sex as she does not lose her live force through her vagina as a man does through his penis and still derive the same benefits as described above with meditation on the seat of I cobra....

    Now I must tell you something I did not wish to, but the oracle commands it. The above practices will lead to great huge strength. How great, how huge? Currently I use the strength of these practices to bench

The Book Of Knowing The Manifestations of Ra *Again*

press well over 400lbs, jump squat using machines over 850lbs, shrug 400lbs. I have leg pressed more than 1400lbs. All using iron plates--free weight. I stand 5'3" at 175lbs. I first benched 300 at 150lbs. But this is only part of the tale, my fearlessness-male strength is untold. My Ra force is incredibly high and literally love to dream of war, conflict and struggle, and enjoy it in my daily life when it seeks me out--never do I seek it out for I know no good can come of. I do all I do to achieve the works set out here and remember to achieve anything even the spiritual takes strength.

    This is the strength you will need to bring about peace--to use your spirit to suffer your friends and fellow human beings to create Maat upon the earth. It is not simply for the sake of orgasm. You want to seize this world from pollutants, defilers, war mongers, to create beauty but your great internal strength is the only weapon you have, for you can never strike an outward blow. Oh, how many times I have tried to relay this...Tantra and other forms of so called sexual kung fu is not simply for the sake of orgasm but for the type of strength found only in myth(which are always only non-christian spiritual stories meant to teach just as the bible is.) And I am always laughed at. Sad, I but so true...

    A last story for the chapter. The legend of the jade pillow book is well known. The jade pillow book is a book of sexual secrets which was given to newly weds in ancient china. One day this book was given to a bride, a noble woman and heir to a throne, by her noble man who loved sex with women. After the marriage unifying territories, the male went traveling the country side to have sex with any woman he wanted. He left his newly wed to ponder the book. While he was gone the woman mastered the book, and through her own actions--sexual misadventures-was disowned by her noble family as open infidelity was disapproved of. The male was caught in the grips of HetHeru's power and became desirous of the largest phallus possible. He eventually under went an operation in which he received a horse's penis. He and his penis soon became a sex slave in a brothel. Meanwhile, his former noble virgin who had mastered the book in his absence was quickly becoming a master concubine (prostitute) with a reputation known through out the land as the Golden Lotus(vagina). After many years of wasting his life force the young man became blind. He sought the aide of a wise man to reclaim his male strength. He was told that only the Golden Lotus could return his strength. Upon seeing-hearing each other they both wept. Some say one killed the other and then his or herself.

    Do I need to say more...?

The Book Of Knowing The Manifestations of Ra *Again*

SIX
THE ORACLE OF RA
Wisdom unlived is spiritual death
The last thing you'll want to listen to, but the only thing you should.
At the feet of Tepra

    Oracles are as ancient as man's understanding of God, the supreme being. There are oracles in the bible and they are a part of many non-christian religions. They are used today in the white house(did you really believe it was just an astronomer?) and in secret by other heads of state. From the ancient Indian Tarot to the as ancient I Ching, the oracles are part and parcel of non-European based religious tradition. Many of these oracles have been used and manipulated by less than spiritually sound individuals to prey upon those of us with less spiritual knowledge.
    No, oracles, when properly used, are not to meant to be used to tell your future. As we shall see, telling the future is virtually impossible. You see, we all have free will. And it is this will which makes the future almost impossible to predict. The oracles, whether they be cards, coins, sticks or little pieces of plastic, are little more than a tuning receiver. What is being

The Book Of Knowing The Manifestations of Ra *Again*

received is a map of things as they are shaping up in heaven, and so on earth. Or better put, with oracles you are being shown how your actions or intentions are affecting your life upon earth and therefore your life in heaven. I tell everyone to consider the oracles as tools to live by which protect your spirit so that you minimize both the harm comes to you and the harm you cause others while you do the greatest spiritual good while on this earth-the only deeds that matter. Now of course this doesn't mean great wealth and goodness won't come your way because it may, but you may have to change how you think to understand it.

In recent years there has been an oracle craze. Egyptian cards, rune stones, and angel decks have flooded the market. Some of them have been presented to the world out of sincere efforts to bring spiritual light and guidance others are insincere efforts to make money. Some are even means to communicate with dark spirits. Yes dark spirits. Ask any oracle system to contemplate itself. It must tell the truth. This is the protection God has granted you. Accept the answer you are given. It may be your only way back to the light.

Each oracle comes out of its' own spiritual tradition. The I Ching of the Tao hopes to guide your internal spirit to the middle way and therefore spiritual success in life while a deck of Angel cards would guide you to the protection of Angels and toward the path of becoming an Angel.

The Ra oracle is dedicated to the spiritual guidance of the vast amount of spiritual power and strength which the practitioner is cultivating. It is specifically attuned and set up to address the inquirer's particular relationship to spiritual challenge which he or she has brought to the oracle within the context of the spiritual system. A simple illustration will suffice; however before we begin let us review this system. Remember our goal: to become God's warrior upon the earth to usher in peace and harmony upon earth and so in heaven. That comes directly from the great story of Ra who fought the Apep serpent in order to lead souls to heaven. To become God's warrior, during the day we must train, discipline our selves within and without--work out and separate ourselves from this earthly world. In a practical way, this means that we overcome all our emotionality, anger, weakness, addictions etc. At night we work on total separation from the world by working on Amen meditations and stretching before sleeping. Don't forget that every morning starts with a Ra meditation. Do not worry, we will review all of this later.

Let us now discuss the oracles in Egyptian or Kamitic tradition. Any amount of research will show you that every Kamitic oracle system on the

The Book Of Knowing The Manifestations of Ra *Again*

market states that it is in some shape or form The Oracle of Tehuti. Yes Tehuti is the codification of wisdom in the Kamitic system or the aspect of God which is wisdom. These decks are being named after the God of Wisdom. The Ra Oracle, Tep Ra stems from the same vein, but is named after the system for a reason. The focus is upon the system and what it is you are being taught--Divine wisdom relating to the usage of the Ra force in the world. Yes, you will find that it could have been called the AmenRa Oracle because all wisdom can be gained during Amen meditation and moments, however the emphasis is upon being told what the wise thing to do with the energy which you have or are creating within you. You will find that after receiving your clarity on any discussion with God--your inquiry of the oracle, you will go into your nightly Amen mediation. Once your usual work is done and you have sufficiently turned your back on the world and have become one with the night sky, darkness, stars, then you will find yourself at the feet of AmenRa. You will look into the sky. There slowly you will find the truth of any matter displayed before you. Beware of anything which you yourself write at his feet by your own hand in your meditation!

Now a practitioner coming before Tep Ra will be instantly told what should be done about a situation he inquires upon given his current spiritual and physical ability. Let us say a man wants to take a woman but receives the Set or Apep and fiends card as part of the reading. Immediately with the Set card the oracle is calling the inquirer's attention to the fact that he has opened up himself to the negative forces of the universe and will consequently suffer--disease or some such. With an Apep card the oracle is showing the inquiry that the people outside of himself--including the woman are such that harm will come from without. You see in the first situation, he himself is the problem and in the second situation the people around him is the problem. The key is in the great stories. Set is the symbol of evil in the first part of the system which the practitioner must work on-- mastery and cultivation of his spirit. In the second part of the system, the practitioner must work on leading or cultivating others and there it is Apep and the fiends which are the evil. Of course, a reading indicating both Set on the one hand and Apep and the fiends of the Sebau on the other would mean openness to evil with in the individual and in the situation all around him or her. A most dangerous situation, but so common in Oz until the Ozian undergoes spiritual study.

As you can see with the Ra oracle, one sees instantly what is within or without you needs work before you proceed or why you should never proceed. Please, please, please, what ever you do, do not test the oracle. Take

The Book Of Knowing The Manifestations of Ra *Again*

the instructions as commandments. The more serious the question, take the answer as serious. And if you believe a question to be light and get a serious answer than the situation is more dire than you know. Do not wait until you have group sex with a bunch of friends where the balance is wrong and do it for all the wrong reasons to realize that the oracle was telling you that as a man this woman will lead to your own rape by a man you've known most of your life or this woman will give you a disease which you will never get rid of and may kill you.

    Let's say that you are dreaming almost every night for a period about planes flying into buildings in New York city. And let's say that during this period you are considering going to New York, though you won't fly there. And that during this period you are involved in a law suit and that you would be going to New York to see a lawyer who has his law offices only a few blocks from the World Trade Center. And let us say finally that during this period you have been consulting the oracles and they have been very clear that traveling to New York was not to be done. In fact while you were dreaming of this violence you believed that the planes crashing into the New York sky line were just warning sign accompanying the strange readings-- serious, dire answers to what seemed just an insignificant reading on travel-- you kept getting. Then one night a few weeks later, you dream of America going to war. The next morning you awake to the sights and sounds of your dreams as you watch the World Trade Center fall and know instantly what the strange readings were about and where you could have been that moment, instead of at home in bed. Now if I did not take oracles so seriously, I may not have been here to write this book. Remember I said that it is not simply enough to do good deeds and live Maat for divine protection but that you must also make wise decisions using oracles like the Ra oracle? Well I know from experience.

    I could tell you numerous occasions where people didn't follow oracles and fell flat on their spiritual faces and just as many where people followed oracles and still fell down on their proverbial faces. The difference is that following oracles means that you will never encounter spiritual failure--though it may mean worldly failure. The two are not the same. Remember that. Why do we use oracles? Say it with me: To keep our spiritual and physical lives safe from harm as we do the most good upon God's earth. We do not use oracles simply for worldly success or merely to know the future. Will you meet a man? Well with a high oracle such as the Ra Oracle the question you will be asked in the strange dire answer you receive may be

The Book Of Knowing The Manifestations of Ra *Again*

that you will, but what kind of spiritual shape will you be in when you do and what kind of life will it lead to?

Now I asked the Ra Oracle what it could show the world and the answer was Aust positive and Atemu (Amen, or Tem) positive. Imagine my wonderment! To understand what was being said let us review a few things. What was Auset's role in the great stories? She wailed for the loss of Ausar and sought him out then immaculately conceived Heru who would do battle with Set! This is what the oracle was saying it could show the world! That and so much more.

Let us understand also one of the great stories of Auset which we had not discussed but which is perfect for discussion here. At a point Ra became sick. By this point, He was the aged God, drooling and long of tooth. Smitten by a snake which Auset herself had fashioned and left on the road in Ra's kingdom. The One God, Ra searched for the God who would aide Him for He had tried and nothing had happened. Coming forth from Him at His behest, Auset cured Ra by knowing if Ra's own name were said along with an invitation for the poison to leave then Ra would be cured. By this time in the spiritual history of the Egyptians, the two great stories stood side by side. Ausar, Set, Heru and Amen, Ra, and Apep. So Auset's role as the greatest magician was well established in the Kamau's spiritual history.

Understand how awsome this is! She gave birth to the redeemer of truth in Heru and cured the awsome victor over Apep and the fiends of the Sebau. Can you not see what a clear correlation this is?!!! What must the world learn if not that? Metaphorically, metaphysically, magically, she is the beginning of the redemption of our spirits from this world and the ultimate cure for our strength ensuring our victory over the forces of darkness, unenlightened behavior. Say it again: the mother of the Redeemer of truth and insurer of victory over evil, darkness.

Now to understand the second half of the reading I must tell you more about the oracle. Do not worry you will learn much more in later chapters and be well equipped to use it. For now however understand that the Ra oracle has several choices to use to communicate the Amen energy. Amen itself, Atemu -properly spelled Atmu, and AmenRa. When given an answer involving Amen the questioner is being told that the he or she must concentrate upon the energies within himself to achieve spiritual power. when given an answer using Atmu the inquirer is being told about the state of the energies--the true spiritual power around him and whether It may be accessed and used in the struggle against darkness around him. Remember it is what Atmu did when morning came and He became Ra. Never forget the

The Book Of Knowing The Manifestations of Ra *Again*

most important part of the battle was the night when Ra returned to nothing (this is just a metaphor for spiritual preparation). Never forget It is the god AmenRa or Atem-Ra not Ra-Amen or Ra-Atem.

So what is the incredible message? Merely that it can help the world achieve the goal of this work you read. It can help create God's warriors and help them weave their strength together and help save this poor besieged blessed tragic place! All this simply by helping to aide them as individuals to redeem themselves and the world's truth and help to pool the vast spiritual strength which can and must be cultivated and created!!!

It's real easy to see in practice. You consult the oracle every way on your road to spiritual growth and when you have attained enough spiritual energy within to control your world and immediate surroundings, and then you can dip in the sea of life safely and participate in the spiritual war for light. Here's a scenario. Let's say a man is threatening the world's health by threat of leading a regime to the brink of nuclear disaster. Only the world doesn't know nuclear disaster is actually on the horizon but rather it believes that individual terrorists' wars will occur with this person and his people. You have redeemed your life and resurrected Ausar within you so that peace and prosperity reign in your immediate surroundings. You read the paper and see the nuclear disaster waiting to happen. You say "ah, Amen--what ever happens-- will." And you let it go. After your nightly Amen work, you sleep. And in that sleep, you dream a ritual to save—he world using your spiritual energy--power and the power of others around you. (Simple visualization of the sick demented man being pushed from power and brought before the Spiritual World Council as Set was or bound as the Apep serpent was during the day.) You go to the oracle and find out that you should participate in the struggle against this man instead of letting it go. After all you are leary of becoming involved in worldly war because war is always anti-human, however you know there are moments when the anti-humane amongst us must be dealt with in ways which will stop them for the good of the whole. After clarification from —e oracle readings, you do the ritual--visualization. After some time, you find that the world stops in its tracks and forms many political and military coalitions to end this threat this maniac has created. Because of the world "heat" this man experiences, he drops the plans and has to run leaving his lackeys and plans for nuclear disaster in a state of ruin.

All over—he world, this ritual was played out--the Catholics, and Christians prayed for peace while the non-European spiritual people ritualized for peace and harmony to save the world by removing an obstruction to peace by bringing forth great and vast spiritual energies.

The Book Of Knowing The Manifestations of Ra *Again*

And you participated in all of this because of oracles. (notice I did not say lead) What's more, you know your participation mattered because your ritual, confirmed by oracles, showed you exactly how it would play out. You don't even laugh out loud, but simply smile when the world reporters discuss the nuclear threat and its plans found in one of this maniac's houses. Because it has all played out just as it was revealed to you.

You dug deep in the spiritual well of the world and used what you were given to help change the course of the world. You who has dedicated your life to God reigning on earth can now call yourself a participant in the human struggle for the survival of humanity. That is what the oracle and system of AmenRa can show you.

A fairy tale? A pagan foolishness? Oh really?

I want you to remember this feeling of disbelief, of cautious interest, but still non-belief. You see if it didn't exist then there would never have been any reason for Oz, Dorothy, Neo and the Matrix, or Alice and the Mad Hatter. However if you do decide to use the Ra Oracle and the AmenRa system, whether or not your spiritual basis changes to AmenRa, an interesting thing will happen each time you attempt to pull someone out of the Matrix or awaken another drifting soul from slumber in Oz. You will be fought tooth and nail, called mad, laughed at and ridiculed. That is what will happen each time you attempt to inform anyone still asleep of the reasons behind your conduct. You will read a story later in this book about a woman whose husband raped her and her daughter. Remember her response. On the flip side imagine saying, "I read this book and now I sleep every night for eight hours, meditate for two and work out for one each day, I'm as healthy as I've ever been, I cure my own health problems, know every thing about to occur around me and no longer care how many things I can acquire." to some one you work with who is killing himself to make all those payments, for the promotions, for the woman or man who could and will care less for him or her when the things are no longer available.... Imagine walking up to an Oz citizen you love with the results of a reading: "I read this book and had this dream then used this oracle. You know you're going to die early because of those cigarettes--why don't you stop smoking?" After you're finished collecting your scattered hurt feelings, you'll realize not everyone is ready to swallow the pill. — SLOW. Give them the book for a present--your reward will be endless, boundless. Participate in discuss with them after they've dreamed. Let the universe slap them. It's easier and probably more efficient.

The Book Of Knowing The Manifestations of Ra *Again*

As aside, this response is mere Set within them fighting to maintain control of their lives. Yes, Oz has an army. Didn't the Matrix? But that is the lesson after the next two chapters.

The Book Of Knowing The Manifestations of Ra *Again*

SEVEN
The chapter of Dreaming a new world
The oldest way of seeing in the book
Of dreams and Oracles

The world is God's dream. God is the dream of Humanity. Both man and God will dream forever or this world is lost. Still we must remember that humanity's dream for this world is not our own. I'll say it again: humanity's dream of this world is not our own.

Many traditional creation "myths", which means just about any other story than Genesis, concern God's creation of the world through dream or vision. Much of the world has been created by dreams more so than we know or believe. I should say that more than you know or believe because I know and I believe. And I know you are starting to see because of the dreams you are having while reading this book or the dreams you were having just before you started reading it.

A crazed maniac sleeps and dreams of ruling the world. Upon waking he is sad, but as the sleep clears and the trance haze--the moments when the world of dream overlaps with the waking world--starts to disappear, he starts

The Book Of Knowing The Manifestations of Ra *Again*

to focus on all the energy of his ego and what he perceived as power which must be ordained by God--for did he not dream it? And do not dreams provide the province of God? He sets about the five year plan of ruling the world. Later he invades neighboring countries and starts world war II only to have his Nazi dream land shattered and his homeland destroyed.

    I used Hitler's famous dream for a reason. He is so far removed from your world that you would be willing to listen to what I have to say. But if you knew what I knew, then you would understand that Hitler is not that far from your world. At night, you sleep and you dream of having a relationship with a person or thing who or which will destroy the family or potential spiritual life you have created. You open your eyes, swimming hard to be awake so you can be happy, while ignoring the emptiness you're feeling. All the while telling your self the emptiness (spiritual emptiness) is no more than tiredness. Now you're awake, being happy because you are being given signs of happiness--good things to come, or simply because you had a good dream—bout something going right in your life--finally, for once.

    Jump switch, two years later. That job or person has destroyed everything you were working on in your life. You stopped your spiritual study, you lost your family. And still you can't admit that that you were wrong. That was no happy dream. It was a warning. I tell you now the emptiness was your divine spirit communicating with you. And why not? You don't meditate to communicate within. You don't meditate to communicate with God. And even if you did, you believe you are told only one thing. "Keep on doing what you are doing my child." (Oh how I wish I could show you how many people have told me: "God wants me to be happy. God wants me to do this." without any independent confirmation from outside themselves)

    But most times people just go on ignoring all the bad consequences of their actions and the forewarning they received. I choose a good dream example because we obviously ignore nightmares about every situation when it is something we want. Do we not?

    I say it now and forevermore just as our ancestors did. The only way to check a dream and the will of God is through oracles. Any thing else is just you running to or away from something that may or may not be good for your spiritual life.

    People dream of other people all the time. Objects, desires, goals float in and out of view. We can not always assume that the people or goals and things showing up in our dreams mean exactly as we may literally take the dream to be. There is a myriad of symbols of spiritual information being

The Book Of Knowing The Manifestations of Ra *Again*

expressed. Deciphering this spiritual information is a complex task that is akin to a spiritual science, yet it is so easy once the oracle is used. Using any oracle ask two questions once a dream is had. Inquire of the oracle what is the spiritual lesson meant for you in the dream and if the answer is not clear then and only then ask the next question: how achieving whatever end you believe the dream or reading to be speaking to would affect your spiritual life. Now understand this may need several questions as you break down each individual section of the dream because sometimes there are many things needing to be corrected in your life. Depending upon the importance of any one thing then you will continue dreaming of it until you have figured out what is being communicated.

Now understand that dreams are incredibly important in spiritual tradition. Through them, you have access to the world you only "dream" of. If you are fortunate enough to have that dream where you are at the foot of the great God you know, please pay attention to it and struggle to understand it. Watch the message play out in your life.

Dreams will also be a way for the spiritual forces in your life to aide you in completion of your spiritual work on this earth by sending you in the direction you need to seek out even when you refuse to walk those roads in your waking life because of the struggle and hardship which we know to be associated with them. What I am saying is that during dream state you are more receptive (able to hear) things which you can not hear or see while you are awake and believe yourself to be right in what ever you are thinking, seeing or saying.

A story: I had a woman, call her Jane, come to me, and referred by another woman who had explicitly trusted my counsel for some time. Now I had given Jane a reading regarding her husband some years earlier.(why is it always about relationships or money or some other worldly thing?-because until there is some spiritual growth there is no other desire regarding which the inquirer wants information) That first time Jane simply asked me to tell her about her husband. After several readings and some trance, I told her that as she believed her husband had been having an illicit affair and unbeknownst to her that he was also going to sexually abuse one child and physically abuse another as well as rape her. (all too common in the spiritually untrained world) Now she became angry with me, telling me she was Catholic and didn't believe in my oracle.

Jump switch-- some years later. Jane calls me at my home. Upon speaking to her I ask her what she needs and she tells me you're so good you tell me. Now I do not like operating like this. Oracles are not toys and trance

The Book Of Knowing The Manifestations of Ra *Again*

energy is precious energy, but I also know that for the most part people do not come to me they are sent because to the spiritually untrained my life is madness, my God is the devil, and I have to be "out my damn mind",--Lord have I heard it all. As a result of my understanding the nature of spiritual forces, I ask the oracle should I suffer this ingrate and give what is asked. At the oracle's behest I do. Jane is naturally amazed when I tell her she is involved in a lawsuit which is probably criminal and she must help impose penalties on one who will not bow to words. So after I tell her that it is probably her husband she is screams in amazement. Of course, it had taken three short years, but her husband's behavior had come to light. He was having an affair with the woman I had told her about and as well he was molesting her daughter--his step daughter and had threatened to kill the step son if the son ever told. Jane herself was now participating in the husband's criminal prosecution as well as the divorce. And yes, he had raped Jane after he was kicked out of the home.

And yes through all of her amazement, I could not help but feel a great sadness come over me. Her life, the life of children in her care had been harmed in almost unimaginable ghastly ways which could have been prevented had she but listened to warnings obtained from a timeless, tested and true source- a high oracle. So often am I confronted with such sadness time and time again after giving a reading. But can I fault them?

They are living as participants in a religion, Christianity, which is not a spiritual system, which has no effective means to help them become better human beings, gives them no divine guidance which is checked by objective tools-oracles, and listen, if they do, only to their own heart--supposedly receiving God's will--or the word of the untrained who have no means to check their counsel in ministers, pastors, and the like. I ask you what pastor could have given her the information I had? And they have been taught to fear what it is that I can give them by the greatest plot this world has ever seen as they struggle through the matrix, in Oz, in the rabbit hole past the looking glass. And each time I come to the moment when the Christian who could not hear me is hurt in the very way which I said they would be I am angry, but not at them. My anger is toward the plot, toward this world, toward Set and Apep and the fiends of the Sebau for they know what they do. For Christians duped by this world I am only sad. As sad as I was for Jane.

Now returning to this woman who had cursed me in the middle of a department store--which is where the first reading had occurred at her job-who had talked about me like a dog, was now my best friend in the world.

The Book Of Knowing The Manifestations of Ra *Again*

She was amazed and grateful for my putting up with her--though she never mentioned it nor apologized, and though she never admitted it, but must have been kicking herself for not hearing me, for vilifying me, if she loved her children and wanted to protect them. But she had hope if she could listen to her dreams.

You see dreaming had brought her back to my door step. I knew this, though I said nothing, just as dreaming keeps you reading this crazy book. Dreaming keeps us all related in the way we n—d to be so that we may grow spiritually--the only growth that matters. Beware of dreams of worldly things without an obvious spiritual connection; the situation at issue is obviously dire.

When I met with Jane at my job, she told me she had been dreaming of mortally harming her husband and his woman and that I would help her. She said—he knew people like me knew such things--roots or some such she called it. After several readings I explained that roots and black magic were lower forms of working with the world around you. That what I lived was not black magic, that the greatest harm she could bring to him was in what she was currently doing and that the God wanted greater growth for her in bringing down worldly justice and forgiving the woman. I explained that this was a pivotal moment in her spiritual life, that if she could manifest the fire and strength necessary to forgive, let go and live, while functioning within the system of justice she was now operating under, then the world would open up and magical powers awaited. Indeed she would empower her spirit so that using it in the world was just a little spiritual training away. Some times, we do not search for the Maa Kheru moment, it seeks us out and if we are alone in this world spiritually without a guide, we must forever be vigilant for the moment when it descends upon us without announcement or fanfare as it had sought out Jane. She would be able to will her spirit to life, if she could live up to this challenge.

At any rate Jane had misinterpreted a dream and oracles, only oracles, clarified her misunderstandings. Did Jane hear me? She has the rest of her life to answer it. When she left me in anger she was in search of someone to give her a spell. The greater question is whether you will listen to the truth when oracles tell you about your dreams. Or will you invade your neighboring countries? Only one can aide you in answering the question and its the same force that could help destroy you. But that force is the next subject.....

The Book Of Knowing The Manifestations of Ra *Again*

EIGHT
HERU
Holder of Amen
Champion of Maat
Grandson of Ra

This is the force that may ultimately save you. A story to illuminate. The place is far, far away, the time is long ago. The evil empire is advancing against the forces of light. And you are a special being in the universe. You understand without anyone telling you that there is an unseen force moving through all things which link them, and once understood this unseen force can be cultivated within and manipulated by you in the out side world. You are approached by an age old order which wishes to teach you the proper ways to do what must be done within you so that you are not taken by this dark side when your understanding of the force makes you only what it must-extremely fertile ground for channeling this life energy. You join the age old order. But you do not heed your teachers who ask you to meditate to control your body's lower passions for love, lust, reckless abandon, revenge, hurt and pain, and all other desires but rather believe your natural abilities

The Book Of Knowing The Manifestations of Ra *Again*

make you more powerful in the force than all these things. By the time the Dark Side is done you have lost your arm and tried to kill your daughter and son, even whole entire worlds before finally losing to the light, as you must, but not before causing incredible pain for untold many.

Just the Star Wars movies eh? What if I told you the Dark Angel paradigm preceded all stories you may know and the paradigm, original upon which all others are based, came out of Egypt within the story of Heru? Sure you probably know of Lucifer and his fall from grace but do you know of Set and his attempted take over of Ta-Meri, Ausar's empire, and even Heru and Set's great fight, Set's attempted anal rape of Heru?(in which Heru cut off Set's head.) All of this written thousands of years before Christ was ever born, the books of the Bible ever created.

Consider this for a moment: Set was Heru's uncle. He was the brother to Ausar. Egyptologist are quick to point out that Set was once a "good" aspect of God worshiped in many ways that the other so called deities were. Egyptologist only wonder what happened to the deity and why It fell into ill repute. What they witnessed is the fall of good into evil, light falling to darkness. The original Dark Side. And we know what took Set there: Jealousy, Envy, Anger. All of the dark emotions which he gave himself over to. Still sure that Cain and Able were the first brothers to visit the Dark Side?

So with that said let us make a small detour and understand the role of spirituality and martial or internal arts for it is here that the connection may be made in the fullest light. I have not referenced another book on any subject so far, purposefully. I do not wish to confuse you. Many of you would seek out the imitation and turn your back on the original; for in this world many have not been exposed to the original and wish to gain by the furthering of imitation. These pretenders have guided the world in the direction. Their poor guidance is truly a case of the moon posing as the sun which can not power your solar battery powered spirits properly. I once gave a good friend a book on Taoism in order to illustrate a point. He now can not hear me about Amen Ra and considers himself Taoist. Not a problem, I can't make someone believe in something, nor is it my wish. But while my Asian brothers created a spiritual system which includes some of Ancient AmenRa when they left Africa, it lacks much of the system and therefore is an inferior basis or foundation than the spirituality of Amen Ra is for Aw-Ra. Understand? All of those sexual secrets reveled in chapter two can be found in many books, yet those books do not concentrate on a spiritual basis so they lack the proper spiritual foundation. Understand?

The Book Of Knowing The Manifestations of Ra *Again*

Now let us talk about the book the Tao of Jeet Kun Do by Bruce Lee who was unarguably one of the greatest internal and external martial artist who ever lived. This book discusses the form which he reveled called Jeet Kun Do. Although the novice and fan alike credit Mr. Lee with creation of this form, in filmed interviews Mr. Lee himself admitted that he did not create Jeet Kun Do, but rather reveled an age old secret martial art. This is relevant only in that I am simply doing the same thing. It true that A Ra is an age old secret form no one has truely practiced it in thousands of years. For you egotist and nay sayers out there waiting to discredit me, I am not saying that I am Bruce Lee. I am merely delineating a point of reference. Now as for Mr. Lee's book, Tao simply means the way. Yes Taoism is a spirituality of the way in life. The first part of Mr. Lees' book is not about hitting a thing. It is about spirituality drawing on sayings, philosophy, the age old wisdoms contained in Taoism, Zen, and Buddhism. Any one not familiar with true Martial arts will not understand why. Mr. Lee was simply showing through the form and function of the book that Martial Arts is merely the external understanding of the internal spiritual system. You can never master any form, no matter what belt you hold, if you do not master the spiritual system. You can not tell me that you are a master of an Asian martial art form, if you have not mastered the Tao, or Zen, or Buddhism. This flies in the face of what it truly is you are doing. And if you wish to argue to the contrary, then you need to go back to the beginning, or someone has lied to you. I don't care how much time you spent in a dojo, how much money you spent and how much technique you know. True masters know, it is not on the dojo floor, but in front of the shrine, in walking life where the true master is created. Belts keep up your pants, and teen age black belts are common and funny at best. (for what internal strength has a child understood?) Traditional martial arts culture--temples and the like-- would never allow the proliferation of pretenders that exists today. You are a master when you embody the spiritual system underlying the form. It is this which makes you worthy of teaching, quicker than any student, stronger than all students you can heal, know what is about to occur, are one with all life...A master of the force that binds all! What you do with your body is merely a reflection of this! If you belong to a dojo and have stayed after seeing your teacher smoking tobacco while sipping coca-cola and eating death burgers that is your fault.

But enough of that truth, why the emphasis on spiritual systems by Mr. Lee in a book on beating someone down? He is hoping that you will learn to control the force that you can become if you use his book. He is

The Book Of Knowing The Manifestations of Ra *Again*

giving you justice, temperament, charity, PEACE as presented by those spiritual systems in the hopes that when you reach the cross roads you will not choose the darkness. I merely took the other approach and hit you on the head with it and I told you about the crossroads which will come using A Ra and Ra because this system will empower the body with so much physical strength that only true power in the form of Amen can control it.

So you say you'll never choose the darkness? Need I remind you that just a little while ago you were asleep and didn't even know it? You are probably living in a little darkness and are quite comfortable. Look at all the dark behavior you allow in your life.

"It's just a cigarette," you say and you deny the obvious that it causes cancer. "It's only sugar," you say and deny the high blood sugar which killed your grandmamma. Pick an ill, odds are because the dark side rules this world, there are several which you participate in. "I don't need sleep."(even though every thing points to a longer life and greater health with it) "I can't live with out meat." (even though it causes heart attack and stroke.) No you don't need a place far away and a time long ago to find an evil empire to fight just as you don't need a Midwest tornado or a looking glass to peer into "reality". All you need is the here and now. And if you can't overcome such small examples of darkness then what will you do when you have much more strength, understanding of the truth in this world and the stakes are so much higher. Will you kill for a nice shiny car, as so many do with their jobs which serve the dark ones?(killing includes helping them sell death) Will you kill for a nice house, more green paper and a prettier woman, a more handsome man? Will you kill your friend out of some emotional anger or other darkness? Or will you turn your back on the world and become stronger so that you may help others grow in life force until the day when the collected life force is so strong that the darkness must once again retreat?

Can you truthfully argue that the darkness does not rule this world today? Set is in the middle of a long and infamous term and the people suffer across the globe. Heru is in training within his Aunt HetHeru's breast awaiting the day which must come for the open war with Set. Ra sleeps and the serpent is in the night sky. Until the day when the Sun is so bright within us all that Apep will loose the battle and Ra will trod upon him for an eon and light of day will rule.

This is just the age old metaphor. It is the spirit of the people which has always kept the governments honest. Look today in China where the depraved Government has repressed and oppressed religions from Christianity to Falun Gong (a quasi traditional religion based upon

The Book Of Knowing The Manifestations of Ra *Again*

strengthening the people through meditation, divine love, oracular systems and practice.) Thousands of people surrounded the Chinese assembly in the square in front of the house of government in simple meditation stance, doing no more than truly peaceful assembly. The people in the government could be no more afraid then they became. Unlike America where the strength of meditation and such has never been shown, China's culture is deep with the truth of spiritual strength in the legends of Kung Fu, etc... The Chinese government outlawed Falun Gong and branded it a cult.

Now I do not know whether it is a cult; for I do not truly know what a cult is, it seems that every spiritual way of looking at the world which does not view a dead Rabbi as God's son and holder of the keys to heaven is one in this country, but I do know what occurred in that challenge in the square. The leaders of Falun Gong had decided that it was time to challenge Set-Apep, of course using the assistance of oracles. In that particular situation, Heru-Ra came from hiding and pronounced that it was over. The awsome hold which Set-Apep has over the good people will not last forever and we may not see it in our life time, but Heru-Ra rises all over the world as I write this. Many will suffer, the way will be arduous, but the light creeps slowly across the globe as health becomes more important than money and slowly the people themselves care more for each other than things. All high Oracles indicate that a flowering of light(Heru! Ra!) approaches the earth, however it will take patience, and spiritual strength and eventually inner spiritual power to make those who will not submit to the law bow down to it and Set aside their inner Set so sharing and love can procreate. **Never must an offensive hand be lifted for the light to reign!** All that said, remember the manifestation of the light being seeded in the slumbering human souls upon this earth are many years from manifestation on a grand level. And this does not mean a spiritual world is automatic. Humanity must choose to wrestle itself from the darkest amongst it. And it could easily choose to allow the darkest amongst us to kill the world before the light returns! We are now at that crux and will be for sometime. It is only through spiritual systems like the one in this book and others like it where the world will find salvation.

Now that we have applied the great story of Heru to the world, let us apply it to the individual. I work with a man in a store. He is big and strong, works out and lifts much weight. His testosterone level is high from years of the right supplements and has been a professional athlete. Homosexual male and heterosexual female customers are drawn to him equally, if they are as shallow as to allow his physical appearance to attract them. What they don't

The Book Of Knowing The Manifestations of Ra *Again*

know is that he is the classic poisoned dragon of Asian martial arts lore, or what we will call the Set up cobra in Aw Ra. Such animals are merely images used to convey the idea of some one who uses the secrets he has learned to serve his worldly self and all the host of emotions. Lord Darth Vader is not just on the screen.....

    Now my coworker chases every woman who looks like she just graduated from high school or who doesn't have grand children, all the while saying that he is single. I laugh while women look directly past me to him no matter where he is in the store. Little do they know, he could truly care less about more than what their bodies can do for his small ego and smaller body parts. You see the man is angry at having to pay child support, can barely stand conflict, has little sense of righteousness, even proud to have sex with another man's woman, married or not; or sex with another man. He has shown up at this place wearing sandals and toe-nail polish. 6'2 290lbs and toe-nail polish! And yes he even knows that he can not control his body when faced with pleasure. He has even admitted that he prays to his Christ to take the illness(uncontrolled emotions in the face of sex) from him. (sadly that is an analysis I've heard from many christian men) Now is this the man they all want? The answer in this society is yes, sadly. Yet this man is illustration of a point. Most know that you must be strong enough to do the right thing, but few know that you must also have physical strength to do the wrong thing. Conversely, almost unexplainably you need vast amounts of strength to do right, and merely some strength to do wrong. It is as simple as that and only becomes clearer when the wrong is done. Let us look at this man for illustration

    This man lacks a Heru level in his life which would allow him to overcome Set, however he has gained enough of that life force so that he may indulge Set in his war with Heru. This is what the great story means when it states that there was a lengthy stalemate. Heru had the power to fight and sometimes was victorious but some battles were lost to the small serpent.

The Book Of Knowing The Manifestations of Ra *Again*

NINE
THE LIFE FORCE BECOMES VICTORIOUS OVER SET
THE REIGN OF HERU IN OUR DAILY LIVES

If this man ever truly turned his full attention to victory over Set--all his emotional compulsion to serve his worldly needs--he would have to use the things which he has learned and turn all of it against himself. All of his discipline, dedication, courage, supplements and workout routine would have to become the discipline to overcome his need for sex and validation, his supplementation pointed at inner strength, his courage to lift more and more weight must become the courage to suffer the loss of conquest opportunities and loss of indulgence in his female tendencies caused by too much indulgence in HetHeru--the over sexualized life force.

THE METHOD OF BECOMING HERU IN
AMENRA ENLIGHTENMENT

In a word, the Set up cobra has to become the Sun and two cobras. The life force symbolized by the sun must be protected by the cobras, the

The Book Of Knowing The Manifestations of Ra *Again*

cobras can not live as a snake! The subject of growth would have to sit in daily sun meditation and visualize the sun and cobras in his seat of the cobra with his visualized cobras destroying the little snakes in the grass approaching him or the Jackass approaching him.(He would see himself actually doing the deed not watching himself) When he became strong enough internally he would see himself walking through the grass trodding on the snakes. Next, he would see himself on the battlefield destroying snakes. Finally once the life force was strong enough he could see himself fighting, then binding the personification of Set the great Ass and bringing him before the world council. This would be the metaphor for his life force overcoming Set.

Understand the stages which are happening here. He is amassing power at first to resist the emotions which compel him while he is visualizing the cobras destroying the snakes. There is no need to let the snakes eat at his life force; for in truth they already are! Snakes eat at your life force each time you choose not to do the right thing no matter what the circumstance. Do not worry your life force understands the imagery occurring. Do not go into trance looking at one circumstance and wishing victory. Use this method of visualizing the snakes and it will guide you to success in all levels. It is a great meditation as well as a meter of the strength of the life force. If the snakes are successful at getting past the sun and cobras in your visualization, then you will not be surprised when you fail to hold the fire in your daily life. You know you are not ready to begin the out ward fight in what ever the challenge before you until you can be successful at every level up to and including bringing Set to the great hall! This is provided that you are successful without forcing the image. It is obvious that anyone can force visualizing something. You must learn to trust yourself to tell the difference.

Once you believe you are ready to take on your challenge you — return to the Ra Oracle and see how you proceed. Ah wait a minute you say what is this about oracles-- you didn't mention it at the beginning of the chapter. Well yes I did. I told you that Heru was successful when he sought out the great Tehuti known as Wisdom. Wisdom taught Heru how to overcome the stalemate at first and again at the end. Wisdom taught him how to bind his uncle then gave him back his kingdom. So too must you. Go to the oracle first to see if you should do a thing then return when all the outward forces demonstrate that that thing may actually happen. Victory may seem like trouncing the enemy, but it may actually, and often does, lie in loving the enemy.

I can't say this enough. DURING THE HERU PHASE OF THE AMENRA SYSTEM, YOUR VICTORY LIES IN GETTING SET(the

The Book Of Knowing The Manifestations of Ra *Again*

forces of destruction in your life) TO THE GREAT HALL. IT DOES NOT LIE IN HIS UTTER DEFEAT.

Just remember this for now. This is the victory—of Heru over Set. It is the victory of you over the wrong in your own life. You can not kill your self--one half of you is the compliment. It is not the victory in the external phase where you are leader of a particular undertaking using the Ra system. There you are Heru Ra Ur and victory lies in the complete and utter destruction of the monstrous Set's guise as the Apep serpent.

What does this mean in practical terms? It means that once Heru has regained your kingdom after taking Set to the council, then you will never be ruled by your emotions again! You will become the crowned King Ausar and all the goodness will flow from and to you. A great health inside and out, flowering prosperity will live in your world! But you will have to give up cookies and cake, you will have to forgo monetary wealth gained by the objectification, persecution, and the exploitation of others which ruins the(your) world! You will have to give up everything not righteous and things not supported by the oracle. EVEN IF YOU CAN OBTAIN THEM! And in this world where Set rules by force and the Divine Love is scarce that means that you will have to give up much.

THE HOLDER OF AMEN
HERU'S GREATEST CHALLENGE IN THE SPIRITUALITY OF RA

Are you beginning to see why Heru is the Holder of Amen? To put it simply, once you have truly achieved the spiritual inner success of attaining Heru upon this earth within your own life force, the greatest challenge you will face is to let go of things which you have been working toward attaining on some levels in the outside world only to achieve inner success. The examples are many. You are called upon to heal the enemy, you once so feared that you had to summon up all your Heru to encounter, now once the enemy is on the run from the great force with in you, you must let him go, even bandage him. You summon up the courage to fight off a lion either real or metaphorical from the front door of your home. Do you chase him alone into the forest? No, such is a losing proposition to any living in this world. Some one has stolen what you believe to be your life's work from you and made millions. You take readings and go to court with him thereby providing him with his last opportunity to do right, Maat, unto you. Unbeknownst to you, he decides that if he loses he will harm your family. You fear him not but not all of your family knows how to protect itself. You dream and know

The Book Of Knowing The Manifestations of Ra *Again*

that God has decided that you will come to a break in your lawsuit which will let him believe he has won and you can back away, you do not appeal a judge's decision. You work hard on your spirit to give up success in the objective world, to stop your forward motion in the lawsuit. It is hard to give up because the oracle readings had supported it. You have firmed your resolve, your Heru level is high. You have decided to fight Set until you have his head in your hands. You want your opponent's head more than anything in the world. But you breathe and back away, despite the readiness of all involved to consider going forward.

Finally, when you can, alone, back away from every one and thing, you smile; for you know that righteousness rules the world and the oracles have indicated that your opponent just signed his own death warrant before Ra by refusing to give you justice and now is on the run. In trance, you are at his judgment and execution, long before you ever pick up the paper and learn of his untimely very early death in the newspaper. Remember justice occurs without our in put we merely expedite it by our actions or in actions for good or bad.

Understand now how Heru as Holder of Amen can save your physical life? Can you also see how it can activate and help you maintain your spiritual life?

Amen is the God of Nothing, no things-right? To live in an Amen state merely means to master (have spiritual emotional strength in) the moment of having nothing in a world of things. To live Heru you must suffer loss in this world--give up the worldly things to live righteously. So how can the human spirit worship, exalt no-thing-ness if it has been raised by the spiritually immature in a land of things? What happens when we as humanity lose things whether they are money, objects, sex, or anything else? Anger, doubt, confusion etc happens. And we go to war, we hate and so much more. Consider the manager who would love to have sex with the mates of others. He would get angry at me when I would tell him that I knew the mates of these women! He told me not to tell him about the husbands of these women and that he has broken up happy homes! Look at his anger when faced with righteousness. This is typical Set behavior.

But what if, instead of allowing ourselves to Feel so much we stopped ourselves from feeling- cut that emotion out of existence? We could what? Do as we must. And in any spiritual system what we must is always become Divine through our actions.

This is the point hidden in the great story of Heru, Ausar and Set: Amen! Yes Amen! What greater test of your ability not to loose your control

The Book Of Knowing The Manifestations of Ra *Again*

and kill the person responsible for killing your father and attempting to rape you! Yes, when Set bent Heru over and attempted his anal rape, Heru did cut off Set's head, but he didn't kill Set.

An aside: anal rape by males of males was a symbol of domination actually used in war for many years in ancient times where male leaders of the victors in war would physically rape the leaders of the defeated openly before all the defeated people, but remember it is also a symbolic spiritual story of how the spiritual light responds to male homosexuality.

What greater test for your ability to be in the world but not of it (Amen) to not kill the being responsible for your attempted rape and stealing every worldly thing--your kingdom as Set stole Heru's birth right from Ausar; for ultimately this is what Amen means. When your body is in the world, however your spiritual state is totally powerful, read peaceful, regardless of the great disaster of the moment you face than you are exhibiting an Amen moment while on earth.

Many say this Amen demonstrated by man is Ausar-that Amen is not personified. However, for the purposes of AmenRa we wish to say this- you are Amen at that moment. Not to be too technical but it must be said: Many will argue the impossibility of actually achieving the nothing state which is Amen; however, it is no more difficult than actually becoming Heru. Remember, it is all archetype and metaphor and in AmenRa, there are personification images of Amen just as there are of Ausar.

Now using the illustration of the great story applied to our poor blind friend who is off some where chasing a woman or, secretly a man, while his world falls apart. He eventually got fired for failing to manage the store and merely being a counter worker more interested in sexual activity than the sales of the store. (yes he will have to seek Tehuti--oracles or wise advise to reclaim his world for he has lost his eye and more) What have we learned? Only reiterated what we've learned from past chapters. But now let us put it in spiritual terms you are now ready for.

HERU OR SET
THE CHOICE IS OURS BUT ONLY THROUGH THE BREATH

Heru is an energy of God which we all have inside us. It is this energy which we use to make the choice to be Godlike on earth or Set, Satan, devil like on earth. When we choose to be Godlike--recreate the spiritual kingdom on earth, we are champions of Maat Divine love. When we choose to perpetuate the kingdom without divine love, we are Set--rapists of

The Book Of Knowing The Manifestations of Ra *Again*

nephews, jealous of our brothers etc... In essence, when we choose not to be Heru, we are all that is not Godly!

We know however that this energy we must put into motion by choosing one way of life or another. Here there may seem to be a catch 22 for the uninitiated. You must fight your emotions as Heru for control over your life, but it is your emotions which stop you from becoming Heru. The key is in the breath (Amen--remember I said it is the breath which activates the Amen all over the world and turns it into Ra force). Once this is strong enough, then there will be no catch 22. There will merely be a thought. "I will be Heru, I will not be Set."

But that breath is strengthened by techniques of exercise and supplements which allow you also to ignore the call for righteousness and do Set's will. You must choose from the outset before embarking upon strengthening the breath what shall be your destination; it will be the thing that saves you in the end. If you choose to live the light of this spiritual system from the beginning, any other path you choose is just you telling a lie to yourself, or becoming confused by the host of other spiritual actors on this planet.

You must fight darkness every day in the Heru or internal phase of study, for it will be your compass. Daily after succeeding in bringing Set to the world council in trance, metaphorical sword in hand mirroring your sword from the Per Ra--or dojo. You will fight that Ass(Set's other personification) so that no matter what manifestation he takes--Darth Vader, anger, jealous— horniness, greed, envy, you will be ready. And remember at night is still the most important meditation with Amen--the crux of Heru and Ra and every thing. For what hold will the worldly emotions of jealousy, anger, even unfettered horniness have upon the spirit which is turning its back on the world?

Now I have not quoted the great wonderful Pert Em Hru (Egyptian Book of the Dead for those of us who don't remember) before now. You see this book should be seen as a companion to that book. There are a great many books on Egyptian spiritual systems out today and some of them have much knowledge which will change the world and they are allowed to sit because we are lazy. Yes, we are the lazy ones! Some of us just don't want to work that hard to become something that can change the world. So I've broken a lot down for us in an attempt to make the difficult easy.

Not to be too technical, because I understand we are lazy, but those books use the Theban system--of or relating to a period when Thebes was the spiritual center in Egyptian history. In the Theban formulation, Heru and

The Book Of Knowing The Manifestations of Ra *Again*

Ausar are the foundation of the spiritual system. And before those of us who know more start to assail me, yes, I know this is quite a broad generalization, but practical only for the purposes of this book. The AmenRa system you are now reading about has Amen and Ra as its center and comes from the earliest periods of Egyptian history and emanates from Annu also called Heliopolis. Additionally, I offer that few other books, if any, other than Knowing The Manifestations of Ra and of Overthrowing Apep dealt with this direct confrontation of evil because of the attending secrecy and nature of the work. Perhaps there is some temple yet to be unearthed which would me prove wrong, but given the awesome strength of the system, I would be surprised to see so much written down for the unsuspecting to find.

All of this said I could not leave Heru without showing you a Passage from the Pert Em Hru(technically translated as Coming Forth by Day by some-but still meaning being awake. By now, it should be clear how awake and day can be interchangeable in spiritual discussion.) After all you may think that I really don't know what I'm talking about, when I've merely taken the approach that most of the Theben system is so well known that it is superfluous for me to add to it. Let us look at Plate XXV or as the book states "the beginning of the chapters of making transformations." It states:

> *I was like Heru, the prince of the Divine boat, was given to him the throne of his father....I passed judgment....I am pure. I have destroyed my defects. I have made an end of my wickedness. I have annihilated the faults which belong to me....I know, even I, the ways secret of the doors of the* **Sekhet-Aaru***(heaven). May I rise up there, may it be granted to me that I may come and that I may overthrow my enemies upon earth, [though] my body buried it is.*

Can that be anymore clear? So we strive for purity, achieve it and become the prince who receives his father's throne. You must be asking how can this be the force which could save us or kill us at the same time? It is simple. It takes great strength to be Heru. But that strength should be truthfully called spiritual power rising from Amen. Power as in potential. Within us is this vast power (potential because it has not been used in the physical realm in our actions). When we unleash it, a number of things happen, it either controls us, we control it, or it is controlled for us by unseen forces. That power is naked, raw energy and we must decide to control it before we unleash it, or we will watch it destroy our lives. You must understand there is only right and wrong, good and evil. That is the truth and which one your energy serves must be decided in trance-Amen and Heru

The Book Of Knowing The Manifestations of Ra *Again*

meditation before it is unleashed or is faced with the evil it can not over come and so bows to it. Consider Plate X of the Papyrus of Ani from the Pert Em Hru:

> *Horus (Heru) it is [when] he riseth up with two heads, one having Maat, the other having wickedness. He giveth wickedness to the worker thereof, Maat to him that followeth after it.*

Darth Vader or Luke Skywalker, Set or Heru, Apep or Ra. These are the questions you must ask yourself. Today, not tomorrow.

The Book Of Knowing The Manifestations of Ra *Again*

TEN
SET AND APEP
Truly the emotional slaughter

Before we begin, let us state a universal truth: God does not care how we live our lives, whether we are happy or sad, wealthy or poor. Worldly success is no indication of vindication by God, no sign of having received blessing, although it may be the result of such. Given the state of the world, wealth may simply be a result of the tricky intellect combined with great will and desire for wealth. This world is currently ruled by Set and Apep's ways, the subjugation of many for the luxury leisure of the few at the expense of all. Naturally, the successful will be those who master that approach to life— Still there are just as many spiritual lessons and rewards for those who live this way to overcome it and live for the many--sharing and truly loving. And there is equal spiritual failure in failing to do so once the truth is understood. Sadly most don't ever know their success or failure until too late. Essentially, having or lacking is not the goal nor issue. Those things we have the opportunity to achieve we desired only for the spiritual lessons in attempting to achieve before we arrived upon the earth. Knowing this truth now we

The Book Of Knowing The Manifestations of Ra *Again*

must have the following one guiding principle based upon Maat- divine love- as the reason we pursue any thing in what is currently Apep's waste land: What I do for another I only do for myself. Every achievement, goal or desire must be honestly pursued for the sake of others. Only true selflessness can protect you from the world of Apep and Set. I will say it again. ONLY SELFLESSNESS CAN PROTECT YOU FROM THE WORLD OF APEP AND SET.

Now let us state worldly truth- emotions and the whole host of corresponding actions are responsible for every problem which humanity has ever experienced.

We put those truths together and we remove the justifications for emotions as well as set the foundation for overcoming them and the problems that they helped create which may yet serve to be humanity's downfall. The only answer to emotionality is un-emotionality or spiritual behavior better known as divinity. Our spirits have no emotional set pattern, any great spiritual tradition will revel this. Whether it be Taoist, Buddhist, Zen or any African religion, true spiritual enlightenment and therefore enlightened behavior revolves around emotion-less behavior.

Let us look first at the worldly truth. Every problem you have is due to allowing your own emotions free reign. A few stories for illustration.

My best friend for many years got caught up in several rage venting incidents over a time. Finally one night he looked as if he were ready to hit my mate for simply walking away from him when he was screaming at me and several of my friends who were trying to tell him the woman he was with was no good. I never "hung out" with him again, despite his apologies for his disturbing the peace of a home and being wrong about the woman in question. (She eventually lied and threw him out in a snow storm, even sported another man's engagement ring within a week.) Once my mate picked up the butcher knife to stop him in his tracks--he was a good boxer at the time-- I knew our friendship was over. He was out of control and life was about to slaughter him. He would be a victim of emotional slaughter. I decided then that I would not be at the funeral or the moment of his death.

He lost a good friend.

This is an example of the emotional slaughter to which Set and Apep lead you. It is emotional because it was his emotions which tore his own house apart. Anger and a host of emotions confused him and slaughtered the good- a friendship that would lead to spiritual development and many other friendships. It is a slaughter because all of that which had been good in the situation was destroyed forever, truly. He had broadened the circle of people

The Book Of Knowing The Manifestations of Ra *Again*

who cared for him, they helped to meet his human needs--he had moved in with his girl friend in a tiny flat which she shared with four other women. It was small but at least it was peaceful away from two brothers who were drunks who lived in absolute filth. In the end, when he was put out on her terms, he had lost all his new friends, his oldest friend and decent living conditions. Imagine what could have happened had he maintained control his emotions....

Imagine the dope addict who could maintain control of his emotional need for the substance killing his life....Imagine the battered victim in enough control to escape. Imagine how many people would continue living as happy members of society instead of the love lost on death row if they had controlled those surges of emotions which caused them to commit the hideous crimes. Imagine...

Yourself. What it could do for you, and how much good you could create if you could only be in absolute control of your emotions. If Set was permanently bound and gagged underneath your control and Heru bowed to Ausar every day and night--meaning that you lived divine law and taught it to others. This is what the Ausar story means in practical terms. Oh, the friends you would have, the peace you would know.

A story. I once called an ancient friend up. This friend was ancient indeed. Our friendship dated back to ancient Kamit. As I started along this path to understanding the spiritual world around me, I told this friend and invited her to achieve spiritual greatness.. The friend ignored my many calls and finally one day did call me back just once in order to tell me that there was no intention to stay in touch with me. Instantly I consulted oracles. I found that my friend was in the midst of Set. Emotional confusion abounded and I had to suffer her and she would regret her mistake. Later she did regret her mistake, but the damage had been done. I never contacted her again and well we fell out of touch. I had much more to offer her in this life time than she could me and can only hope she reads this book to start the path which was meant for her in this life time. Had this sun bound and gagged Set, what a great destiny awaited.... What a great life and spiritual growth. What a role in the battle with Apep.....

Ah, but before there can ever be growth, there is a war and a battle. The battle against Set. You stare Set down each time your emotions come into play, for good or bad. You must grow so that no emotions are a part of your decision making process and that when you act, you do so because it is what you should do. Heru and later Ra always does what he should. Perhaps an illustration will help.

The Book Of Knowing The Manifestations of Ra *Again*

You are rowing in the smallest of boats in the ocean. Of course the waves are constantly high and you are tossed about constantly. But you survive. Here I come motoring along in a super tanker, literally the largest ship on the planet. Those same waves that toss your boat don't even affect my ship.

The waves are an image for the problems of life and the emotions that we believe accompany them. It is only a belief because truly no emotions reside in our problems. That envelope with the tax bill is not sealed with an emotions potion that infects us. We open it and we allow our heart to go thump, our hands to shake, then we scream at our loved ones, we jump off the roof. But the tax bill was only a piece of paper. Today I open the tax bill and I see a piece of paper. It was not always so. The difference is once I rowed in the tinniest of boats. Today my tanker moves through life, I feel very little. The difference is peace. That is what the big boat is. It is created by not caring one iota for what happens in this world at the very base of your being. The motor moving my boat through the waves is my breath, the awake meditations I use every moment of the day.

Yes, the Amen and Ra stance meditations create a super tanker and the motor. You will sail on the sea of life instead of drowning in the waves of life. You won't even have to surf, go up and down with the waves; instead you will plow right through them. The bigger the wave, the bigger your boat and motor will become.

Now let us discuss Set himself again. He is within us all as Heru is. There is no great story concerning Set. We only know about him through the great story of Ausar and Heru. Remember it was Set who was jealous of the natural order of things and was led by his jealousy and greed to take Ausar's kingdom. It was Set who was challenged by Heru and eventually was defeated, but not before Heru moved through many spiritual challenges. Heru stopped Set from raping him anally and cut Set's head off. This is the spiritual image for maintaining a natural order of things. No it is not all right to steal, to lie, to put a penis in another man's rear. Finally, after the long struggle and contest Heru sought out Tehuti, divine wisdom, and brought Set to the great counsel of Gods. After the case was presented, the AmenRa led counsel determined that Heru would have day and Set would have the night, it would be up to humankind to choose either. By now I don't have to explain this imagery or tell you to breathe and stay awake to choose Heru, I don't have to tell you that title the Book of Becoming Awake, the Pert Em Hru (Heru), is based upon this very story. It is no doubt an instructional book on how to maintain Heru in the face of Set or Ra in the face of Apep.

The Book Of Knowing The Manifestations of Ra *Again*

But why so much discussion of Set in this book about Knowing the Manifestations of Ra again? Is it not obvious? Heru and Ra are one and the same. Ra is simply Heru doubled. To know Ra you must know Heru. The two different stories-books- are merely ways to understand the same energy. The closest way I've come to explain it is an analogy using team sports which are at the same time individual sports. When I was on the Judo or wrestling team in college or high school, each individual would compete in their weight class, and then the total team score was taken. My school could beat another if we won four out of seven matches. Well that is a lesson in Heru. Each spiritual combatant must have the strength to beat their individual opponent. If we were to understand this in terms of the AmenRa Enlightenment then what we would be saying is when an AmenRa spiritualists are dealing with a Heru issue, each one is dealing with a Heru issue within his/her life while fighting Set,(ie he/she is fighting his/her own inability to tell the truth to his friends, to share, to overcome foods which harm his/her temple/ to stop using trickery and deceit in his life...etc.) Now if we indulged in combating under the theology of AmenRa spiritual framework one individual must be able to beat each member of the opponent's team individually or all at the same time.. That is the Ra leading the souls to heaven. Does that make sense? The theology of Amen Ra predates the worship of Heru and Ausar by many years and the aims became different for many complex reasons. But now at any rate you are ready to understand why Heru, Ausar, and Ra are often equated in the Kamitic spiritual texts.

Now let us understand Apep. If we were to draw a spiritual image of Apep, then we would be discussing a foul serpent big enough to eat skyscrapers. We are talking about a huge snake. This is an image of the evil of the world joining forces and creating a dark imposing force more powerful than it was when the comprising forces were individuated. Where ever you find the glyph for Apep, it will be a large snake with spears stuck in every one of its folds. The message was immediate and simple: death to this thing which causes death.

Ever try to defeat evil that has seemed to draw arms across the world and is into everything, indeed it is every thing? Then we are talking about Apep. Apep is the Matrix itself, not the individual robots together controlling it; it is the Empire itself, not lord Darth Vader or the Emperor and all their evil minions together. Do not misunderstand what I tell you. Apep is not the government, but the corrupted life force itself of which the government or Matrix is merely a manifestation. Apep is the corrupted life force which is

The Book Of Knowing The Manifestations of Ra *Again*

everywhere and in every thing when darkness is high. And conversely, Ra is the illuminated life force everywhere and in everything.

Now look around you. This is a period in world history when Apep is high. The darkness has enveloped the world. Sickness, disease, pestilence, want and much more pain and misery are what abound and all that is light must hide for fear of being obliterated. The world is one big giant emotional cloud, a dark, dark cloud. But let us look closer at the darkness that envelopes the light which we cast upon it. Understand there is so much darkness that even darkness can be made to look like the light. Take something very simple like the human diet. The world wide diet is primarily carnivorous, meat eating, on the one hand and many well respected communities recognize the danger to the human body in meat eating on the other hand.(they recognize that the human digestive track was not meant to accommodate meat and that eating certain kinds leads to heart and other disease). Now darkness is so thick that all of this is recognized but eating less dangerous meat is endorsed globally, not a vegetarian diet. The different meat growers associations smile on while people get sick and die in denial saying that it could not have been the meat everyone is eating it.

We are not calling the meat growers association evil. They are confused, in so much darkness. That Darkness is Apep. World wide and growing daily.

The light which will stop Apep is the next subject...

The Book Of Knowing The Manifestations of Ra *Again*

ELEVEN
THE CHAPTER OF
KNOWING THE MANIFESTATIONS
OF
RA
AND OVERTHROWING APEP

Here we have come to the crux of the matter. No more fanfare or introductory matter is needed. From just the glimpse of what Ra is which you have been exposed to up until now what do you expect this chapter to be filled with? Spells to ward off the devil Apep? Tips on how to know when you see Ra?

Well if you need information on either of those then you need not read this chapter and you should reread all of what you have read until this point.

We are speaking of mighty Ra here. The back breaker of the foul. Life! Health! Strength! Itself! There is little more needed to be known than the following which is the secret of Ra. Pay attention or you will miss it as so

The Book Of Knowing The Manifestations of Ra *Again*

many have when the Egyptologists have read all of the ancient Kamitic works up until this point. Say it aloud as you read it to place importance upon it. "Ra (Life!Health!Strength!)"

Again: "Ra (Life!Health!Strength!)

The only true secret, the only thing hidden, here is that life is actually Amen. But that shall be the next chapter in this book. For now let us review what we know of Ra so that we know the manifestations.

The original book of Knowing the Manifestation of Ra (more like a short statement by today's literary standards) which you will find sometimes called the Egyptian legend of creation discusses the creation of the world as told by the God Nebetcher who calls Himself many different Gods from Auseres to Khepera to Nu.(Hidden in this is the point that there is only one God with many names) He is called the One god. You would find this legend of creation in the midst of spells against snakes. (Is there any wonder?)But let us look at the key to every thing and it comes at the very end of the Book of Knowing the Manifestations of Ra and Overthrowing Apep. Speaking, the One God states:

> *They invoke my name, and they overthrow their enemies, and they make words of power for the overthrowing of Apep, over whosehands and arms AKER keepth ward. His hands and arms shall not exist, his feet and legs shall not exist, and he is chained in one place whilst Ra inflicts upon him the blows which are decreed for him. He is thrown upon his accursed back, his face is slit open by reason of the evil which he hath done, and he shall remain upon his accursed back.*

Before we go any further, this is very important. What is the word of power? Note what is invoked. Ra is invoked! It is the word of power! Ra say it in trance, say it going to the store, walking the halls! Watch the change in your world!

That said, understand that aggressively taking on Apep is the secret to the manifestations of Ra! What would you look like in a world filled with the foul serpent if you constantly defeated it by throwing it upon its back and slitting it open? Consider it, what would you look like if you defeated all evil around you by not allowing any poison into you and never settling for less than absolute truth, divine love with your friends? Why you would be a strange bird indeed. More than human, you would appear animated by life force others only dream of. You would be super strong with a super powerful will, invoking the name of the God Nebetcher who in turn is truly every aspect of God from Ausar to Ra. Remember what it means to

The Book Of Knowing The Manifestations of Ra *Again*

overthrow the serpent. It means that you must do away with all evil within and without, but both those evils can only be fought within. This internal and external fight is what it means when it is said that words of power are evoked and enemies are overthrown and the accursed serpent receives the lashes meant for him.

Name the myriad of evil in the world, it is the Ra force which overcomes it. Smoking? Ra force defeats it. Murdering dictators? The Ra force defeats them. It is all one and the same. How will you know the manifestations of Ra when you see it? No evil will be manifest in Its presence!

This is very important. What is the word of power? Note what is invoked. Ra is invoked! It is the word of power! Ra- say it in trance, say it going to the store, walking the halls! Watch the change in your world!

Surely, any resident in Oz reading this would say that is not possible, for no resident of Oz can envision a world without the illusion of evil being powerful. Certainly few believe that big tobacco and big oil can be stopped, that people can be awoken and that soft drinks would be abandoned for water and on and on. However, remember they have not made the long trek toward the manifestation of Ra. Upon the day, they have completed the journey anyone who knows the manifestations will never have to ask. One who has made the journey will always know. Can you envision the manifestation or are you chained to Oz beneath their electronic amplifiers, in Oz's created and self perpetuated ill health, doomed to accept the certain destruction and decay of the physical earth and the desecration of the greatest power man has been given by God-the ability to do acts of Divine Love to the world and all that is in it.

If you at the point where you don't even have the imagination left to envision the world of Ra than perhaps Oz is all that you will ever have and it is up to others to evoke the name of Ra and wake you up along with the rest of the world.

The Book Of Knowing The Manifestations of Ra *Again*

TWELVE
AMEN:
TRUE POWER REVISITED
Herein lies the secrets

    Now we come to a major demonstration of why the spiritual systems of the Kamau were said to be mystery systems. You open the book it says "Knowing the Manifestations of Ra." You believe you are dealing with an understanding of strength as you see instructions on overcoming great evil. Those who don't know, believe this is it; those who know, wait for the moment when the power absolute, contingent upon nothing else other than Itself, shows Itself. Confusing? Good. And if that isn't confusing, then you are a long way toward a path that must be showing true peace and prosperity in your world.

    You see to demonstrate Ra strength you need to be as physically fit as you possibly can. Hence the strength of Ra is predicated upon something other than the spirit with which you were born. However, the true power, as in potentiality of strength needs only the spirit you were born with. Understand however much that may be true, there is one proviso, which is

The Book Of Knowing The Manifestations of Ra *Again*

huge and upon which the strength of the God of Nothing—Amen—with in you rests. To the degree that you can reside with, inside, beside the God of Nothing is the degree to which you will demonstrate strength in your life.

Here is a spiritual equation that has lived in humanity's varying spiritual systems for as long as there has been spiritual life: Spiritual strength which is the ability to complete or initiate actions in the world is contingent upon Spiritual Power. Spiritual Power is contingent upon nothing other than peace within the spirit. A huge caveat is that spiritual peace is spiritual happiness.

Repeat after me: No thing can ever make me powerful and only Nothing will make me powerful. Take that into trance contemplate it forever and ever and may you see the Sun in the midst of the blackness of stars before the nothing which over takes you.

Poetic, no doubt but what does it mean? Well in essence it means that using the Amen mediation work provided herein which is no more than sailing the stars to the sun and then sailing the void into nothing but blackness you come to the nothingness which is Amen and that is the sea of life flowing through everything in the universe. To the degree, that you maintain contact with this is the degree to which you will exert strength in the world. Now you have found the Power of Nothing. Mighty incredible Amen from which all other things of the universe flows. The creation of the universe and the destruction of the universe rests within Amen! Read any of the temple text which have been translated and you will find that the greatest power in the world will be attributed to Nothingness. It is called by synonym Nu, Amen, Atem and so many names of "Gods" which have survived through time. Even with the Destruction of the world discussed in the Book of Knowing the Manifestations of RA, it is Nothing which is most important and discussed first. Said the God Nebetcher, the Kamau's name for the entirety of God: "I was ONE by myself... I made all the things under the forms of which I appeared then by means of the Soul-God which I raised into firmness at that time from out of Nu, from a state of inactivity."

Understand it this way, nothingness is more than the way to the power, It *Is* the power. Nothingness within the spirit will allow the spirit to become manifest as power then strength, remembering that power means only the potential to do a thing.. This is the most important understanding of this chapter. What is nothingness? It is Amen. And when there is nothingness in the spirit, what is there for humanity? Only the spirit by subtraction; for some thing must remain or the body would no longer dwell on this plane. If you dwell in nothing, then what is there? You, meaning your

The Book Of Knowing The Manifestations of Ra *Again*

spirit, and nothing else. It is entirely difficult to attain and has been called much by many, from hetep to nirvana to the middle way to nothing again.

Are you starting to understand why dark blue is Amen's color in the AmenRa system? Understanding why the void of space, even space itself is a part of the ancient Egyptian's spiritual representation left behind for us to find; why space is a part of the dreams? Space represents nothing, and nothing else. If you are successful in achieving nothing, no- thing –ness, during meditations you will perceive nothing—black, hear nothing, feel nothing. This, the perception of nothing, is supposed to be impossible according to western science, but it is the summit for which spiritual masters have reached and attained through out life times. Calm will be your state upon exit and life will begin to become easier and the degree to which you can carry your calm, your sip from the cup of Nu, Amen, Atem is the degree to which you can exert The Power in your waking life.

Let us take any given activity to understand this very important point. A person afraid of losing their job because of poor performance becomes emotional, angry and nervous. This person's performance suffers even more because of his agitated state. And the inevitable happens. This person is fired. Now take another person, same circumstance, however this person has tapped into Amen and in his calm he is able to not only do his job, but do it well. What has happened. Pure spirit has walked through his calm and controlled his world. Choose any individual task and Amen can succeed through you. Period. I said period. Walk on air? I said period. Money from thin air? Period.

Period?
Period.

The Book Of Knowing The Manifestations of Ra *Again*

THIRTEEN
The AmenRa Approach to Achievement
The Daily life of the Useru

Let us refocus before journeying any further. This book is an introduction to spiritual cultivation of the modern day Kamitic warrior. Yet that does not mean that the AmenRa system is only for people who are in the military or who are martial artists. Everyone is at war in their daily lives to become a better, read spiritual, human being. This has been true in every millennia since human kind has drawn breath. But if you have been attempting to live as a spiritual human being on this planet lately, you realize how difficult it is no matter your walk of life. You suffer physically from a host of ailments, you have no peace, you have no vitality, you have no happiness, you have no will. And all about you there is so much that threatens your world and the entire world. You should be under no delusion; this moment in time is more dire than all of the previous put together. *We are at a cross roads and the darkness descends upon the four corners and moves toward us. Opposition to peace and spiritual enlightenment chokes the world as you read this in ways it has not before nor will it again in many a millennia, if the enlightened win.*

The Book Of Knowing The Manifestations of Ra *Again*

Bold words and daring assumptions you say? No, just the reality for any spiritual being with oracles and awaken eyes to see.

Understand, there is purposefulness behind the devitalization of food and water. There is a reason for nuclear proliferation.

Christians would say the "Debil" is strong. Kamitic spiritualists would say Set is on the rise. This Kamitic teacher of spiritual combat is telling you that Set has become the great Apep serpent, its scales entwined in every last thing meant only to devitalize your opposition while feeding upon you.

Understand I say it is purposeful, but that does not mean that everyone serving Apep does realize it. There are those in the darkness that have been there so long that it is the light which is foreign to them. There are few, but they do exist and they are in the highest worldly places, who know that eating that beef and indulging in so many of the weakening pursuits of this world is helping to keep you in darkness and enslaved and feeding them worldly wealth. Only by becoming and helping to create a light in the midst of the advancing dark can the great serpent be thrown upon his back and his face slashed by means of his own evil....

This is no easy task. I say again, this is no easy task. And it is a way fraught with so much danger to yourself and others. If you make your appearance as a light before you are ready, than darkness will seek you out and swarm about you and none shall see you.

This book you hold in your hands was written years before it was made available as it was being updated constantly. No wise warrior enters an optional battlefield without being ready. I held myself back using the great wisdom of oracles in order to be the vessel ready for what publishing this meant. You see the tendrils are in everyone everywhere and I will seem foolish but to so few. If I were not ready for the idiocy I am sure to face for saying that smoking is from "da Debil," then I may doubt myself and fall into the advancing dark.

THE AMENRA APPROACH TO ACHIEVING IN THE WORLD

This is obviously so applicable to this chapter. It is the number one rule we must discuss. While working this system, err on the side of caution and hold yourself back before action. We will call this the Amen (lack of action before) Ra (action in the world) approach. During the lack of action you nurture your spirit in meditation and fitness until action. Here you will envision possible opposition and success over all of it. Hold back until you

The Book Of Knowing The Manifestations of Ra *Again*

believe yourself ready, then hold back again, until and only when the oracles say you are ready. If you do not follow this method, I guarantee you that you will be eaten half awake, half alive, by the great Apep serpent as you follow the world to your spiritual doom; for you will be only half ready to achieve what you will and Apep will feed deeply upon you until one day you are back in the Matrix, in Oz but now you will find yourself leading and recruiting for the darkness because AmenRa training strengthened you to the point of leadership, but your will serves the dark. A little application may bring this to light.

Let us say that while impoverished and struggling I am brought to my knees to pray. "Lord." I ask, "Make me a tool so that I can be financially successful, and bring light to the earth." Ok nothing wrong with that. The next day I am hit with this very book, visited by incredible inspiration. I write the book like mad and I want to put it out there immediately to relieve my perceived suffering. Long story short, I'm not ready and I focus upon the wealth and not the whole point of the work so that I have just given a doorway location and become lost in the process. Now I turn around and simply rehash the same things in very tired ways in sequels. And to make matters worse, I chase the Emperor's coin so hard that I start to simply tell people what I know they want to hear, "morality is situational," or some such. "Oracles are foolish." And lastly, yes, you knew it was coming, I read another book of wisdom and I parrot it, pretending it to be my own and the darkened people hail me a…..motivational speaker….new age thinker….best selling spiritualist…..I'll even have my own mystic whom I'll say I met at the beginning of my journey who told me to write this….

Sounding familiar? Flashlights who are the moon reflecting the hidden sun are far too many in this culture. Today you have decided to have your eyes upon a comet leading you to the sun. But you too will one day be a flashlight and will know that you are but whether you continue upon the path of enlightenment, follow the comet's path all the way to the sun so that you are drawn into and become a part of that sun so that you may illuminate humanity's darkness depends upon….

Amen. And whether or not you held yourself back at every necessary moment. You must understand in a very short time of following these spiritual practices, a mere matter of weeks for some of the cleanest amongst you, you will have more energy to do what ever you will in the universe but your will is not pure. And spiritual purification is no more than the process of leaving the world to the world. So what you serve until you have been purified truly is this world and by extension- Apep. Yet remember, you will

The Book Of Knowing The Manifestations of Ra *Again*

not know that is whom you serve and will curse every other spiritualist who attempts to bring you back to the light. And all because you were merely a flashlight who could not listen, who dared, who ran past readings from divine oracle systems.

Meditations and exercise are done on an empty stomach

To meditate, sit with back straight, eyes forward so the line of sight is parallel to the floor or ground, hands upon the thighs or knees on that body part's side. Standing meditations will be offered later. Close your eyes and simply breathe as you fix your mind upon nothing at first. These meditations are so strong; your body will become so pure using the daily regime that the situations and energies will come to you eventually.

Daily Spiritual Practice of the Useru. (Initiate)

Stretch

The night before the day of the beginning of the spiritual practice, the Useru must stretch the body then enter into trance.

Alter Creation

Clean the alter by wiping it down with pine soap and a clean cloth. Kneel on your right knee, head down, right fist upon your chest, fingers over your heart, left hand in a fist at the end of the arm bent to form an L facing you before the chair or alter in which or before which you will meditate and say *Enui En Ra Ennuit Htef Xennu Amen...Ra!* These words are from the Book of Becoming Awake and entreat Ra to enter in and clear all obstructions within and without.. In this way, you are using it as an invocation, an invitation to spiritual forces around you to enter your space and aid in your spiritual communication within and without. You will bow in this way before every formal communication with God. A depiction of a variation of this bow occurs at the beginning of this chapter.

Rise and hold any object to placed upon the alter and say the word Ra, or AmenRa while visualizing bad energy leaving it. Next, sit before the

The Book Of Knowing The Manifestations of Ra *Again*

shrine with your eyes closed and feet flat on the floor. Breathe at a comfortable rhythm with your eyes closed.

Meditation

There is only one meditation done at night. The Useru will see all the objects of his desires leaving him or walking a long hallway past closing doors of rooms filled with problems, temptations and the like and or herself riding out into the stars or toward his/her understanding of AmenRa. The goal is to let go of every desire want or need. Do not worry as it will seem difficult at first; for you will be afraid because of your worldly training. You will want to keep every thing. Be mindful of all your physiological responses—chest heaviness, muscle tightness, any sort of response to what you are seeing. Eventually you will achieve nothing but peace—the lack of tension in your body, mind, and spirit. This is important as it is the start and end of your power you hope to gain.

You will sleep deeply and your spirit will consider all of what you have thought was your limitations in your dreams.

Morning:
Daily Meditations

The Useru is held to rising early and meditating hard. Meditation must be performed within the first hour of waking. If it is done more than an hour later, the Useru is too far removed from Amen found in sleep to get the best meditative work. In your meditation, you will be continuing the work of the night before so there is a necessity to go into a "woken" trance as soon as you awake. Such a stringent requirement is loosened the more time that the Useru has worked mediation.

There are only two visualizations the Useru strives for during the morning meditation: absolute darkness (Amen) and letting go of worldly things as well as the sun becoming the *solar* plexus also known as the torso (Ra). After the sun has become part of the torso, the Useru will see himself/herself being successful with active goals such as making money and physical achievements. He or she will see herself as hawk headed doing this. For the last part of the meditation the Useru will see darkness and letting go of the very things he saw himself be successful with. This is very important as the Useru wants to strike the balance of spirit between what is to be achieved and the Amen of it that must be mastered. **WARNING.** If the

The Book Of Knowing The Manifestations of Ra *Again*

Useru does not finish the meditation in Amen state of letting go what is desired or worked toward, then his energy to achieve what is willed or desired may become so strong as to be hazardous to his and another's health.

Surely, one can see how dangerous the Ra meditation is. What you see in you mind may be what you desire. So you must be sure it is what you should be getting. Only oracles may provide that information. So until an oracle is available to the Useru, the Useru must be content to visualize working out, extreme fitness goals and simple wealth for his family-- *not the things themselves* but see and understand you and yours around you as having a glow of prosperity at the foot of a hawk headed Ra. This simple visualization will help you from running afoul in the wrong pursuits.

These are the simplest most basic meditations to be done. The Useru will evolve eventually to mediations previously discussed in this work as in HetHeru and Ra specific scenarios and which will be more fleshed out later in coming volumes.

Daily Physical Exercise and work of the Useru.

Work and work out hard while avoiding Set's food during the day. Here is the Useru "earns his money" in this system. You must remember the spiritual rules regarding the relationship of the strength of the body to the spiritual strength of the spirit. On the whole, the greater the strength of the body the more spiritual power which it may hold. This is truly a generalization because there are so many factors at either end which may affect this potential including violations of so many spiritual laws discussed up to now. For example, an individual might be physically strong as the strongest person in the world, but he or she does not suffer for, does not sacrifice for, or does not love Divine Love. You do not need the spiritual Ph. D. to understand that this person will not have much spiritual power to wield in the world, regardless of how much he or she may want it.

With that said, the daily physical practice of the Useru must center upon the performance of physical goals dedicated to the improvement of physical strength using spiritual means.

Here the Useru must enter into the actual activities of his goal during the waking moments and advance toward their realizations using spiritual means. Special care must be made to use one's burgeoning internal spiritual strength being acquired during mediation. That is to say the Useru must take the inward spiritual strength building in mediations and mindfully focusing them during the activity.

The Book Of Knowing The Manifestations of Ra *Again*

A story. I decided that I would use this system to bench press 500lbs. At the time of dreams and meditations which initiated this goal, I weighed one hundred forty pounds could barely bench press 135lbs and hadn't gone to a weight room in quite some years. It was clear that I needed to do this thing and everyone I would have told would have told me I was out of my mind. In fact, some did.

Still, I persevered. But it is not the achievement of the goal which is the focus. In fact, I failed. The most I ever flat benched was 410lbs with out a spot and 465lbs with a spot while I weighed 195lbs because of weight gain instructed by the oracle. I lost the only student I trusted with that much weight above my head and so the goal disappeared to the Amen Fields of my dreams as many of yours will if you practice this system. Now, it is the method and the growth of achieving which should be the focus here. While under the heaviest weight, before I pushed it up, during the deep breathing where I summoned the strength to push, I fell into trance and saw myself as the mighty Hawk Headed Heru Ra Ur fighting Set and the great serpent Apep. It was during these trance moments that great clarity came regarding the use of so much of my strength. At times, I also saw the movement of the energy within me to move the bar above me. I saw the energy as bright yellow or white moving from within me through the bar and up. During these times I saw so much of what has become the basis of my great labors of my life up until this point in my life, so much of the future, of the past…Today I use the physical work to run really fast. Down to 165lbs, sprinting has become my joy again and during the sprint work out, my focus time between reps is spent in my mind at the foot of Great Ra where I am shown good sprint times and much more about my life and projects.

What you must understand is that it was not the weight lifting, is not the running which was making me stronger or is making me faster. It is the Amen work which contributes the greatest power to my core base of power. Projecting this power against the world through the breath which is the human converter of spiritual power to spiritual external strength, I was able to do as I wanted or more correctly "willed".

I purposefully did not use a martial art example to explain the above principles. Yes, this is a system of health which is the basis for martial art, but the practicality of martial art in today's violent bullet and bomb laden world is questionable at best. It is more practical to understand that most people reading this would be better served if they applied this to whatever they tried to achieve to maintain their health. In subsequent books which focus more upon the martial aspect of the system, physical strengthening exercises, I will

The Book Of Knowing The Manifestations of Ra *Again*

show exercises which are martial specific and which will hone the Useru's ability to commit miraculous feats of martial art or physical achievement. Should one so chose, one need only use a little imagination to create the exercises i.e.; ten punches a second on a training bag, hurling a punching bag through the air, blocking without seeing, moving without moving using the same techniques expressed above, leg pressing over a thousand pounds, running world record fast....

    What should really be understood is that A Ra is a health management system. You are honing your spiritual strength and making it stronger. This is all for the moment when you need to close your eyes and save the world, heal a little boy or girl, or create wealth where there is none. All by simply digging into your spirit.

    A word of **warning** here. The Useru must pay close attention to the limitations which were set in the Amen meditations before the Ra state of the day. If you remember, during the night before and the morning of the day when he she would achieve, the Useru sat in meditation and let all worldly desires go so they would not control him. Protect yourself. This must be adhered to; for there is the danger that the Ra force within may become so strong that all danger signs are ignored whether it be signs of injury or potential injury. *I can not say this strongly or highlight it enough.* Protect yourself and set limits before the undertaking is started because once trance is begun and you start your spirit will feel like it can take the body through every and any barrier and it probably could but at great cost beyond the foreseen. The obvious one is that you exert yourself too much the day before your intended performance moment or you attempt too much without the proper protection—others to operate as they should at the appropriate moment. As an example, today I can bench press only sets of three hundred pounds because I have no trust worthy spotter. I once attempted to lift great weight with out such and my spotter did not listen to my instructions and did as he wanted to. I tore my lower stomach. It took some time to heal it.

    The same goes for the daily working life. Because this society is what it is, the Useru will no doubt turn her large desire and will—both of which will be made larger by practice of this system (***which will be like oil thrown on the fire of your will, wants, and perceived needs***)— toward the worldly desires of financial and other success. I say this with no qualification and set it off so that you do not forget and are able to easily find it when need be.

    YOU WILL DESTROY YOUR WORLD AND HARM OTHERS

The Book Of Knowing The Manifestations of Ra *Again*
IF YOU ARE NOT ABLE TO KEEP YOUR DESIRES, WANTS, AND WILL UNDER THE CONTROL OF AMEN.

We have discussed this numerous ways, many different times, but it bears repeating here. You see, your Ra work will make your will, your desires so strong, stronger than they have ever been before. And if you are not meditating, using the provided Amen meditations, then you will be a slave to them and your life will be destroyed before you even realize you have shackles on. You must use the Amen meditations provided and none other. Do not confuse yourself and thereby guarantee your own failure by mixing and matching meditations systems. Do not use the Ra and avoid the Amen. No other meditation will cool the heat of Ra or maintain the balance necessary to keep your world functioning in this world once the might of Ra has been accessed. If you fail to use it, as so many have, blame only yourself when your life is in a flaming ruin and you are all alone.

List of Ra Violations

This list is not complete; there are as many violations as there are Manifestations of Ra. This truly is just an out line. The Useru should use it as an initial check against his behavior. In every case, the proper corrective measure is Amen meditation focusing on releasing the subject of the violation. For example, if uncontrolled anger or will is the subject of the violation, then the Useru would go into trance feel herself become hawk headed and trod upon snakes (emotions) then drift into space and see the subject of his anger drift away from him toward AmenRa upon His throne. The Useru's world would then turn to blackness.

VIOLATIONS OF RA
Failure to:
Live the law
(consider using the 42 Admonitions of Maat until you have a grasp of oracle systems)
Discipline one's self (spiritually, emotionally, physically)
Discipline others when needed
Exercise
Eat correctly

The Book Of Knowing The Manifestations of Ra *Again*

Signs of violations:
Uncontrolled anger
Ignorant self willed ness
Hardheaded
Inability to listen to guidance.
Constant disputes
Lack of friends
Ill health
Irritability
Keeping the "wrong company"
Lack of motivation
Vacillation (not being able to decide or constant waffling)
Lack of strength

If you have been following me, then you know that Ra is Life! Health! Strength! Therefore, anything that is contrary to life, health, and strength is a violation. You may ask yourself why a lack of friends and keeping the wrong company is a violation of Ra. Think about it and the answer is clear. Is not the eye of Ra, Maat? Divine Love. And what divine love can be lived without good and just friends to share it with, to be one with?

I offer these here as violations only to recognize that the Useru will be amassing great strength. She will be as a flashlight which will draw seekers and light drinkers alike. He must know what is being done with his Ra force and by whom. Does the Useru wish to be caught up in Jesus Oz using his Ra force to lead using minor Useru tricks of healing and psychic ability because they are weaker, she is stronger and trained? Does the Useru want to be at the top of foul corporations making deals to pollute the earth and bilk the masses because she has a greater grasp upon life? In every case the answer is a resounding No! What are the violations of Ra? Every violation against life, health, and strength. Do not come to me saying you have no violations against Ra when you consistently and knowingly breach the peace of your own home thereby violating life and health of yourself and another and possibly others; when you consistently wish to do what **you** wish to do in spite of guidance by all other sources of wisdom which you once followed before you found this issue **you** decided not to follow an oracle or wise counsel about. You will be left alone yelling to no one that, "I speak to God, I can hear him…" You must understand that you will have the will, the strength, the courage, to stand on your own, even if you are wrong, even if

The Book Of Knowing The Manifestations of Ra *Again*

you would kill your own self, if you use this system to enliven your Ra force. It will be your true friends and God who will say, "I tried to tell him, I tried to help her." One need look no further than the many examples of the fallen from Darth Vader to the once and mighty servant of Ra, Set, who fell to disgrace, for Illumination. Remember that Set was once depicted destroying Apep, the enemy of Ra from Ra's own boat while Ra looked on. What happened to Set between then and when he became the arch enemy of all that is good and just? His own will, his own anger, his own lust, his own greed, his own strength and the refusal to discipline himself so that righteousness, Mighty Ra, could reign in his world. Please listen because sometimes you don't get to live again, sometimes the repercussions are too severe, and lives, including your own, are changed irreparably forever.

I have mentioned the 42 Admonitions of Maat as a possible source of coordinating ones understanding of the law. They are the codification of the Kamau's ancient moral code and have received their just due in scholarly and traditional theosophical discussions. The Useru should consider using it to discipline his spirit strongly until she has understood the Tep Ra, oracle, which will be provided in book two of this series.

If this is just too much and too technical at any given moment merely remember that one must live humbly within the bounds of the law. If you violate this principle, it will not be pretty when the Great God decides you have done enough. Using the system of this book, you will have been given advantages over your fellow human being and full warnings about the consequences of abuse. Become a fouled cobra and suddenly the system may not work for you. You may even forfeit more than your job.

A story. As I've said, I use this system to run very fast. Some may not agree, but I was a slow sprinter while I rounded myself into shape. I worked hard, melted away pounds. Then one morning I woke up and I ran with Ra's wind. I had run so hard that my times were among the elite speeds of men twenty years my junior. I had been as strong as men who were supposed to be among the strongest upon the planet now I was as fast. I had flat benched 225lbs more than 35 times which broke the NFL combine record for my weight—which wouldn't be hard since I weighed less than 190lbs. Now I had been clocked at a shade above 6 seconds in the 60 meter dash, the race for which I was training, which was close to the world record and it felt effortless as if I wasn't even trying to run fast. It was magical, it was ritual, it was the moment when the meditation had empowered my spirit to the point of achievement in the world.

The Book Of Knowing The Manifestations of Ra *Again*

Now at a point when these were easy to achieve once the cyclic preparation time had been given due consideration. I had arrived. I was achieving the great labors of Heru Ra Ur while upon earth. But one day I got injured and on that day, all my speed was taken from me. It felt as if I was running on sand. I saw something I never thought I would see, someone caught me and ran right by me. I finished the race in a very pedestrian shade above 8 seconds. I cursed, mad at the injury. But there was no doubting the spiritual origins of the injury.

You see I had healed every injury using Great AmenRa's strength while training to run. The same strength that made me fearless, fast and courageous, I knew, kept me injury free on the field of battle. This was distressful to say the least.

Jump switch to two months later. I was still fighting the injury. No amount of Amen blackness nor Ra Solar healing meditations had worked. I was becoming worried. I had never not been able to heal something within my own body since the days when I first found the rudiments of this system with my first martial art teacher some twenty years earlier. Still I didn't dream. Oracle readings were clear that this thing would fix itself. But my season was almost over and I had missed meet after meet. One morning AmenRa decided I was ready for the truth. I closed my eyes and saw....

Myself as a black cobra!!!!!! I had lost my way. Ego and arrogance had replaced my humble truly self denying ways. I had gotten into what **I** could do. What **My** feet could do. How fast **My** two legs could move. My confidence had been replaced by arrogance and I cared for the briefest of moments about what the world of men thought about **Me** more than what I did before God with Her ways. And it was all taken from me.

Shocked, I cried inside. Not for the wasted time, but that I had come to that point to need the lesson. I decided then that I wanted to only be healthy and run before God. Very little else would enter my mind, ever again.

Once I understood the problem, it was time for research. I looked deep into my spirit and found the source of my problems. One day I found the slight beginnings of fear at the start line. I over compensated for that fear and it fed itself because although I had conquered it in my daily work, it was still there. Do you know how I knew? Running fast was never something I took into Amen meditation!!!!!! I held to it, clutched to it. I would not see myself running slow or losing. Afraid each time it started to flash before me in Amen meditation, I drifted to something else. And after a while, God stopped trying to put it there. I would not learn from with in so I had to learn from with out! And all God was trying to do was help me because, and

The Book Of Knowing The Manifestations of Ra *Again*

say it with me, if I could let go of running fast then I could only run faster. Running would cross from the physical to the spiritual world of magic where my performance would not be held by rules of cycles and times and ages and such. **Remember this, every thing you strive for must be balanced by Amen or the world will crush you, Ra will desert you and only Amen will be there to wipe your tears, eventually.**

WHAT YOU FEAR IS WHAT YOU STRUGGLE TO TAKE INTO AMEN MEDITATION, BUT THAT IS THE THING THAT MUST BE TAKEN THERE FIRST, FOR TRUE GROWTH.

VIOLATIONS OF AMEN

Amen violations at first blush appear to be less severe, then expected but on closer inspection, they are just as serious. Once again, I must remind you that to say Amen is to say Ra, that the two are the same. When one God is contemplated, the other is as well. There is a silent "Ra" which follows "Amen" just as there is a silent "Amen" that precedes "Ra." One does not exist without the other but for human beings to communicate about the Endless, about the Infinite One, there must be some differentiation. We review this because some of the very violations and their manifestations may seem very similar to those listed under Amen. What is the focus is their origination within the spirit. Ultimately, only Tep Ra, the AmenRa Oracle may be its final arbiter or an oracle of equal measure. For now, we are left to human definitions, such as they are. Remember this is no where near a full list and merely provided to give a vague outline and general understanding.

Violations of Amen

Failure to:
Let go of the things of the world
Live unemotionally
Nurture the proper emotion dictated by oracles or the will while letting one's reactionary feelings fill the moment.

Signs of violations:

The Book Of Knowing The Manifestations of Ra *Again*

Inability to sleep at night for a long rested period of at least seven to eight hours straight with little interruption
Inability to meditate, think deeply
Inability to be at peace regardless of the circumstance
Holding on to negative emotions
Consistent upset brought on by desire to obtain or control any thing
"Thing desire" controlling actions-it does not matter which thing causes the desire, only that a thing has caused it.
Wanting to left alone, wanting to go live alone without humanity.

While it is probably difficult to understand how some of these violations and their manifestations fit together it may not be if we start back at the beginning. What is Amen? It is the God of nothing. So if one were embracing nothing here in the world what states of expression would one search for? Any state where one experiences nothing, no emotion, no desire. In a word, nothing exists for us at peace, in sleep, in meditation, lacking sensual stimulation from the world.

Just as with the violations of Ra, no Useru can say that he or she is in accord with Amen if they are driven to sell life killing legal over the counter prescription drugs to pay the bills. They have not let go of the things of the world. No Useru may say Amen lives within if they are caught in thing desire whether it is a desire for a person or green pieces of paper.

IN THE WORLD BUT NOT OF IT
DAILY LIVING AS A PRACTICAL MATTER

Daily the Useru's spiritual identification must be with AmenRa as accessed through Heru or Heru Ra Ur. Such identification will give way to balance tipping his heart toward spiritual practice. He will be in the world but not of it. It would be unspiritual to fail to recognize the need to exist in this world. The human body and spirit has needs of shelter, companionship, food and the like to live and grow which is the only reason we are upon earth, not to collect things and brutalize, dominate, and destroy with our presence. What must be struck is the spiritual balance of meeting these needs without harming the spiritual storehouse which the Useru is honing daily. Instead of selling evil chemicals, the Useru must find the fortitude to work for less green paper in a job where no one is injured by his actions. She would use her cultivated Ra to work perhaps a more physically demanding job while at the same time using Amen to let go of dreams of the possession of things

The Book Of Knowing The Manifestations of Ra *Again*

that the spiritually incorrect job and all of the attendant Setian or Apep like culture capital, i.e., let go the fancy car, mansion, maid, the need to dominate, and achieve which drove the behavior. To be sure a prosperous life style may be maintained. What must be understood every waking and sleeping moment is the true spiritual price of things. One must never love things, one must never lose sleep over things, and one must never harm oneself spiritually over a thing. In a few words, the Useru must be ever vigilant in Amen against the return of Set and Apep in the world of things.

The Useru has lost his job? The Useru can not get that promotion? The Useru wants to make millions? The Useru wants the wrong man or woman? The Useru wants to break God's law to obtain...any thing? The Useru must remove himself from the world at night and meditate upon nothing, specifically laying representations of such desires at the foot of AmenRa upon his throne. The Useru must remove himself from the world during the day while still working and doing during the day and visualize the sun in his/her solar plexus. It does not change no matter the challenge. The answer is the same. Amen and Ra. AmenRa!

By now you should understand that during the day and in the midst of everything, the only emotion one should feel is the one which one desires. And one should only desire positive emotions of happiness and peace. To be sure there are pressing moments of tension, seriousness and the like in human experience during the day, but the Useru's challenge is to find an unemotional powerful peace in those moments and that peace can be best achieved with walking awake meditations in the midst of it all—Book of Knowing The Manifestations of Ra Again meditations! The evil one within you is thrown upon his back and slit open!

Let me be clear so that this book does not cause car accidents and stock market crashes. I am talking about your emotional identification. How you feel inside. I am not telling you what to think about. You must and should be concentrating upon your job at hand, whether it be family or professional while it is at hand. But all of us have had moments of undesired emotions at every given moment. The Useru must bind those emotions using the above meditation for simply as long as it takes. The Useru will find that with proper meditation time at night and in the morning, the Knowing The Manifestations of Ra meditations through out the day will become very brief until the moment when but a thought defeats the emotion.

AmenRa Daily Foods and Colors

The Book Of Knowing The Manifestations of Ra *Again*

Amen's colors are what? Do I need to tell you? Of course they are dark blue and black for the night. And these can be highlighted by white, for the stars in the sky.

Ra's colors are obvious. The multiple colors of the sun. Reds, Orange, and yellows. Even white, as in white hot. And therefore which color do both have in common? White!

Maintaining these colors during spiritual exercise will help the Useru achieve the desired states of being. If the Useru wishes to maintain balance, he should stay away from combinations at the extreme end as in black and white. The Useru will find the effect of these colors too severe upon her spirit before she has amassed some ability within the system.

Now for the purpose of differentiation during study at the PerRa, martial art temple, the Useru should wear white or yellow. Females who have female health concerns may use dark blue. The Sesh, adept or teacher of the individual PerRa may wear red or orange.

There may be times when the Useru wishes to eat the foods which would help him achieve the desired states. Amen's foods are bland and unseasoned, Ra's foods are hot and spicy in their extremes. You desire a lot of Ra? Eat hot and spicy. Remember to be aware of health concerns regarding foods and spices as they affect the human body. You will have great strength but don't jeopardize one iota of it because you like the taste of salt or sugar and will not feel its bad effects. You may not get high blood pressure because of your metabolism and work out regime, but you will be sacrificing spiritual and physical achievement, still.

Lastly, **avoid all stimulants**. Let your morning exercise wake the spirit and personal temple. Remember any stimulant will only jump start what has already and is already being fire started with in. It will be a double fire situation which can be almost impossible to handle for the Useru just starting out. Judicious use of herbs according to health needs may still be sought out. The Useru should seek oracle counsel and perhaps a trained professional, if she is not certain.

Daily Service to the Community

Ra's eye is made of Maat, the pyramid text is said to say. So too must the Useru's eye be made. You must see Divine Love everywhere, in every human interchange. The Useru must raise the level of the fire and space to give so that all may be given to the Useru from humanity then unto the Useru from God. What is given to the Useru from humanity is the only thing

The Book Of Knowing The Manifestations of Ra *Again*

that can be given by humanity, the Useru's own humanity in a sense of compassion and oneness. Once achieved, then God will give the great powers of that love in the Maa Kheru proclamation.

For that day and only that day, the Useru must choose a needy situation and give unto it. If he or she is helping to build a PerRa, that is a perfect means to dwell in Maat; for a properly run PerRa would only be shaping up to serve the world. The Useru must remember to guard her energy well; for there are many un-needy and simply greedy individuals or organizations that would simply take advantage.

DAILY PHYSICAL ENERGIES WORK

We have discussed the dangers and positives of sexual energy work and they are codified here. The Useru will feel a great increase in daily physical energies after the following when combined with the other sections of this chapter. Remember the goal is to produce as much testosterone and estrogen, growth hormone and the like that we possible can naturally. Scientifically we know the glands of the endocrine system and the hormones they release influence almost every cell, organ, and function of our bodies. The endocrine system plays a major role in regulation of mood, growth and development, tissue function, and metabolism, as well as sexual function and reproductive processes of the human body. Life! Health! Strength!

While keeping your mind clear of all thoughts-

The erect phallus is rubbed with a hot herbal paste combined with a cool lotion and then "pumped" using a male pump.
Daily stimulation of energy meridians within the body which relate to life points of health which can be learned from any acupressure book and will be discussed more in book three of The AmenRa Enlightenment.
The Useru must tap and squeeze each one of the individual testes at least two hundred times.
The Useru must make use of an egg or ball twirled within the vagina or an warm to the touch natural lotion or paste about the opening such as peppermint.
This must all be done without orgasm.

The Book Of Knowing The Manifestations of Ra *Again*

While these activities may be used as sources of pleasure, the Useru must understand and never lose sight that she is awakening her life force to be used to achieve her ends not to achieve an end. All care must be made to avoid abuse. These exercises should last no more than one half hour and be done with as little enjoyment or emotion as possible. It is difficult at first to achieve but will become easier over time.

A word of advice. Since the Useru is cultivating his or her sexual energy and so much has been documented herein as to the great dangers of such, then it is suggested that no new sexual partners are taken on for at least a year for the sake of all involved. The Useru must have this energy under control before it is trotted before the world or he or she will wind up being the ones trotted before the world. Toward that end, THE USERU MUST TAKE HER DAILY PHYSICAL PRACTICE INTO AMEN MEDITATION.

In this meditation, the Useru sees herself or himself laying the objects of physical desire down and walking away male, female or object. Do not worry about the effects of this, you will be able to perform well when the time warrants it. What we are preparing against are moments when your drive becomes too much.

The Book Of Knowing The Manifestations of Ra *Again*

FOURTEEN
The two stages of AmenRa Enlightenment
Sesh and The PerRa
The Sun, The Moon and The stars

Let us remember that this is an energy management system. Herein you have been told what to do with your energy for spiritual, physical, and emotional success in one of the most brutal and fearful times in human history. As such you must understand the energies around you, Apep, the energies within you, Ra, and the energies of the spiritual universe which you may use to change either, Amen.

Consider the chart below and I promise this will be the last such review for you Dorothy, Neo, and Alice.

Apep= all around you destroying you and your world with negativity.
Ra= within you awaiting an empowered will to come forward.
Amen= within and all around you awaiting your Ra energy imposed on a decision to overcome Apep.
Amen+Ra= the positive energies within the human spirit.

The Book Of Knowing The Manifestations of Ra *Again*

Set=the negative energy in the individuated human spirit.
Set+Set+Set (nth)=Apep=the negative energies of the human collective is Apep.
Amen+Ra(-) Set= the Useru.

Simply stated that is the goal. To enhance both Amen and Ra in the human spirit while subtracting Set, the negative principles within the human spirit to create a purified Useru.

To achieve that purified state the Useru undergoes two different stages in the AmenRa Enlightenment system. In the Inner or Heru stage, the Useru looks to up his own AmenRa force by using the physical work out and meditative approaches described previously. In the External or Ra stage, the Useru becomes Sesh, a guide, an instructor, and works helping others to become a purified Useru and on behalf of others uninitiated in the system.

Let us not be fooled. Becoming Sesh means service. It does not mean ruling. The modern day Sesh is no more than the warrior priest of AmenRa walking in today's light. It is the responsibility of the Sesh to provide a place for the Useru to hone his spirit in relative safety as well as a community for her to live what has been learned. Perhaps you would like to call this a church, yet that would be wrong; for this is not a religion. Perhaps you may want to call this a temple, yet that is too limiting as well. This place is simply called what it is; PerRa—the place of Ra.

But why is it not called the PerAmenRa? Only because the emphasis lies where it is. You see in the place of Ra, the Useru learns to channel, to discipline, to use that great Amen which has been turned into other worldly Ra force which could destroy her and those around her. From the very beginning, the Useru must be schooled to understand that it is the Ra that is being externalized which is being offered a place in society. In short, while Amen empowers the spirit, it is not the misunderstanding of Amen which threatens the world, but the misuse of Ra which may destroy all and everything.

And yes it is my goal to regulate all and every PerRa which is started as a result of this book in order to watch the health and well being of every individual who reads this and decides to make the long trek home to AmenRa to be used to restore peace without the rumor of war upon this planet. But it is not my goal to start a religion, church, house, or society. Other than buying the books of this series, there should be no money required to practice AmenRa Enlightenment. BEWARE OF

The Book Of Knowing The Manifestations of Ra *Again*

COUNTERFITS who demand your allegiance, money and or time and wish to teach the principles within these works using ancient names.

Fittingly, let us end with a story. Before I put the AmenRa way website up almost two years ago at the time of writing this, I looked at every site available discussing Amen and Ra in order to see what was out there. Not to steal, but to see if any one had come to the understandings I had. The oracles were pushing me to drop this bomb and I held back so desperately because I wanted to be sure. I taught by invitation only and watched the change and wonder which AmenRa brought to the lives of Useru as they came and went, even as they buckled beneath the incredible challenge of the system.

In my search, I came upon a site discussing only Amen and purporting to put forth the living of Amen from a Nubian perspective. It discussed Amen and nothing but Amen as their spiritual basis for line after line. It struck me that their spiritual work was short, their understanding muddied by a lack of true Amen work. Their obsession with Nubia told me so.

Jump switch. Almost two full years later, perhaps less. My website is getting hit, a lot. I'm getting requests for this book you hold in your hands. I go back on line because of inner emanations and meditations. I return to the site and now these same individuals have not changed their name, they still are a temple of Amen, but now they have warrior training, shield creation, but they use their ancient names.

I smile. I go directly to oracles. I select the ancient I Ching as it is most handy. I ask the oracle to confirm that their perspective was stolen from my site and was told that I was right but to drop it. I proceed further to how to handle it and was lead to what you have read.

You see there are many pretenders, many moons driven by their own egos to attention and money. And if these people can not do what it is they say they can or want your money for nothing, then it is not true and they endanger the people that come to them and themselves.

God doesn't belong to just Nubian peoples, black people, or purple people. No person living AmenRa Enlightenment would believe that.

My anger was great as I entered into meditation and sat before AmenRa. "Let me handle it my child." I heard as the great God grew hawk headed.

I fought myself to let it go. This could be nothing more than Set and Apep and of course, there was one force to handle it.

The Book Of Knowing The Manifestations of Ra *Again*

Now, you must remember what I have told you. I expect many more imitations once this is released. Simply live the way, That is true AmenRa Enlightenment. Any thing less is simply small minded people with smaller spirits who are the moon. When you come together, it is only to hone, to discipline, to experience as a group in a PerRa which needs only maintenance fees at best. If there is to be respect, let it be the Sesh for the Useru for having the strength to leave the world but still be in it, not the Useru dripping unconditional respect and support for a life style and way which he or she is still learning.

Now let me answer the question most of you have. Why is my presentation of AmenRa, *the presentation of AmenRa?* I could tell you of my dreams of binding the great Apep serpent dreamed long before ever understanding what it meant and had years before I began my study. I could tell you of so much related to this system and the growth in my students and others using these principles, as much as I've told you of the disasters of some of them. But what I will tell you is to listen to your own dreams and understandings as you attempt the practice prescribed herein daily for simply thirty days and see your power and strength change in the world seemingly overnight.

Lastly, there are many warnings here. Please attempt to live them. The circumstances which give rise to them are all true.

May this book open the door to the sun and the stars as it was meant to do.

And let us all hope we find the power and the strength each time Set and Apep come to our lives; for only then will our lives and this earth be a better place for all.

Ameeeeeeeeeeen…..Ra!

The Book Of Knowing The Manifestations of Ra *Again*

Appendix
Basic Meditations
A way to spiritual purification for the Useru

In every meditation, the Useru may use physical, spiritual, and mental health images. For example, if the Useru wishes to stop smoking he may close the door on a smoky room. If the Useru needs to discipline himself daily to meditate, he may place an object before the feet of AmenRa which symbolizes his failure to do so or may see the Sea of Life being infected by things which keep him from meditating and watching unsightly characters half man half animal—the Sebau of Set—walking from the sea to devour him. Once she becomes accustomed to meditation, the Useru will find that her spirit is quite imaginative. Readings should be done upon their meaning if it is difficult to understand. But in every case for every cycle of meditation, the Useru should be focused on purification—letting go of all worldly emotions, desires and identification. Each meditation visualization should be done for thirty days without fail for success. During the day the Useru should strive to behave in a way to reinforce the meditation, ie; not smoke if smoking is being fought in meditation..

The Book Of Knowing The Manifestations of Ra *Again*

1. The Sea of Life

Close your eyes and breathe normally then try to see nothing, total blackness or whiteness. Amen is the God of Nothing. You are attempting to see this, to become a part of it. No thought, no sound, no smell, no taste, nothing. You will notice that you have meditated when you "awaken" and slowly feel energized. You will notice that time has no meaning. You should tell yourself before closing your eyes that you will stop in about an half an hour, for normal meditations and longer if so desired. After some time in the darkness or whiteness, you may find yourself drinking from the Sea of life or a symbol involving water, cup, tributary, river, etc. Note what is in the water, if it is anything other than pure life giving water, be warned. You are being shown what within you obstructs the way to life giving Amen. Visualize aunks coming from the water into the mouth for healing.

2. The Foot of AmenRa

Close your eyes and see nothing. Then suddenly see AmenRa, a man upon a thrown with a huge two feather crown and solar disk atop that. Lay at his feet those things which symbolize worldly worries or cares then kneel before him. Listen and feel intently to any messages you receive. They should be all about how you violate your own spirit by holding to these things of the world. Be warned. Any other message and you are not receiving instruction. You may be repeating things in your spirit to be shown how false they are.

3. The hallway

Close your eyes and see nothing. Suddenly you find yourself walking a long hallway filled with doors to rooms. You know that behind these doors are the things which tempt you or are symbolic of earthly desires. Close the doors willingly as you walk past them. Feel yourself dressed as mighty AmenRa. Pay attention to the doors and their attendant worldly symbols which are hardest to close. They are the ones which hold the "traps" for you which will keep you from purification.

Basic Ra Meditations

1. Sun and two cobras over a snake.

The Book Of Knowing The Manifestations of Ra *Again*

After Amen work above is done, the Useru should reflect on her objective then see the solar disk in her torso. Then she should see two king cobras come out from the sun. She should then see a snake(s) approaching. The sun's rays burn the snakes while the cobras kill the snake. If the snake is huge and can not be defeated, the Useru must understand that she is not strong enough to handle it. It means that her emotions are stronger than her internal will and she should be wary of attempting to project spiritual work or the intended objectives of her spiritual work in the real world. She is not yet stronger than the spiritual evil she fights whatever it is. For example if the objective is not smoking and she chooses destroyed cartons of cigarettes as her symbol but can not defeat the giant snake emanating from it, then she is not ready to be around people who smoke. But be warned if you constantly are seeing the snake defeated but are continuously smoking during the day, you have not gone deep enough within.

2. The Sun

The Useru should look at the sun and then be come a part of the sun. The sun should in turn cast a cleansing healing upon all it touches. The Useru should see all pain and suffering leave the world and feel the same within her. The Useru should visualize aunks leaving the sun in front of her and entering the body for healing.

The Book Of Knowing The Manifestations of Ra *Again*

Notes:

The Book Of Knowing The Manifestations of Ra *Again*

Notes: